The Land and People of

FINLAND

PORTRAITS OF THE NATIONS

The Land and People of ®
FINLAND

by Patricia Slade Lander
and Claudette Charbonneau

HarperCollins*Publishers*

Country maps by Eric Elias

Every effort has been made to locate the copyright holders
of all copyrighted materials and to secure the necessary
permission to reproduce them. In the event of any questions
arising as to their use, the publisher will be glad to make
necessary changes in future printings and editions.

Map on page 37 is adapted from the original by Lauri Mäkinen
in *Facts About Finland* (Otava Publishing Company, 1987).

Map on page 94 is reprinted by permission of William Heinemann
Ltd Publishers, and taken from *The Political History of Finland*,
translated by David Miller.

THE LAND AND PEOPLE OF
is a registered trademark of
HarperCollins Publishers.

The Land and People of Finland
Copyright © 1990 by Patricia Slade Lander and Claudette Charbonneau
Printed in the U.S.A. All rights reserved.
For information address HarperCollins Children's Books, a division
of HarperCollins Publishers, 10 East 53rd Street, New York, NY 10022.

Library of Congress Cataloging-in-Publication Data
Lander, Patricia Slade.
  The land and people of Finland.

  (Portraits of the nations series)
  Includes bibliographies and index.
  Filmography: p.
  Discography: p.
  Summary: Introduces the history, geography, people, culture,
government, and economy of Finland.
  1. Finland—Juvenile literature. [1. Finland]
I. Charbonneau, Claudette. II. Title. III. Series.
DL1012.L36   1989   948.97′034   88-27144
ISBN 0-397-32357-3
ISBN 0-397-32358-1 (lib. bdg.)

10 9 8 7 6 5 4 3 2

Photos are often harder to locate than "facts." Hannu Vanhanen, a photojournalist at the University of Tampere, not only opened his own extensive collection to us but served as an ongoing photography consultant during our stay in Finland.

Many individuals from the Ministry for Foreign Affairs, the Finnish Tourist Board, the National Board of Antiquities, the Ministry of Education, the Finnish Embassy (Washington, D.C.), the Consulate General of Finland (New York), the Finnish Mission to the United Nations and General Headquarters of the Finnish Defense Forces, the University of Tampere's Department of Sociology and Social Psychology and the American Studies Program, the Finnish-American Chamber of Commerce (New York), *New Yorkiin Uutiset* (New York's Finnish newspaper) and Columbia University's Uralic Program encouraged and aided us in writing the book.

Press Counselor Eeva-Liisa Elomaa, Commander Markku Moisala, and Professor Samuel Abrahamson stepped in at crucial moments. William and Margaret Lander read every word. We alone, of course, are responsible for our mistakes. Thanks to all. *Kiitoksia!*

Contents

THE WORLD

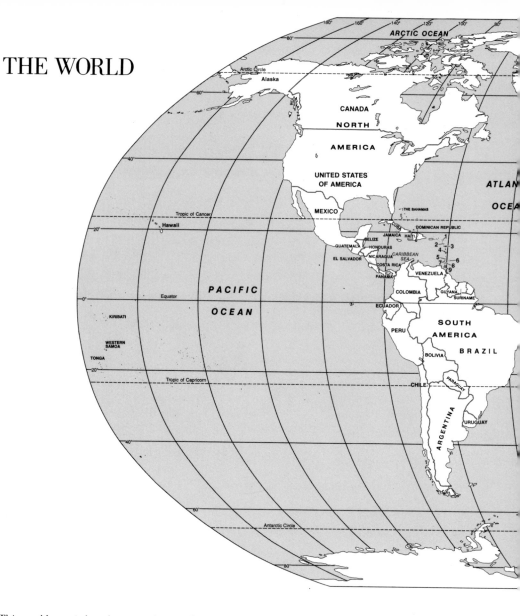

This world map is based on a projection developed by Arthur H. Robinson. The shape of each country and its size, relative to other countries, are more accurately expressed here than in previous maps. The map also gives equal importance to all of the continents, instead of placing North America at the center of the world. *Used by permission of the Foreign Policy Association.*

Legend

——— International boundaries

--------- Disputed or undefined boundaries

Projection: Robinson

| 0 | 1000 | 2000 | 3000 Miles |

| 0 | 1000 | 2000 | 3000 Kilometers |

Caribbean Nations

1. Anguilla
2. St. Christopher and Nevis
3. Antigua and Barbuda
4. Dominica
5. St. Lucia
6. Barbados
7. St. Vincent
8. Grenada
9. Trinidad and Tobago

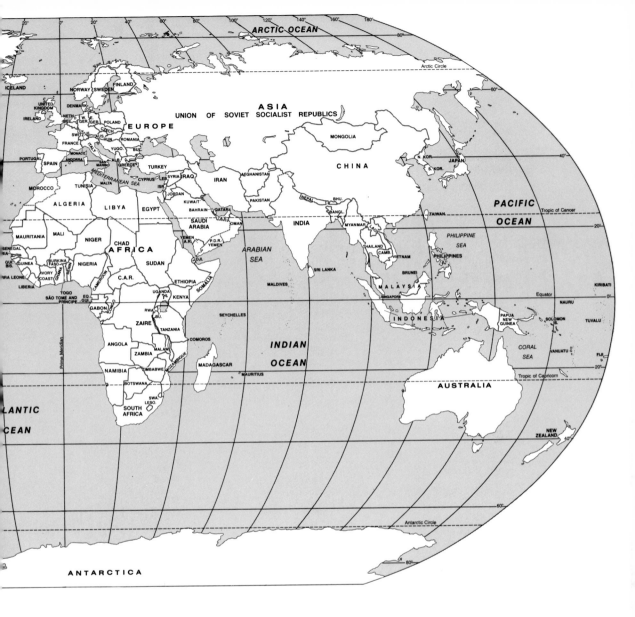

ARCTIC OCEAN

ICELAND

NORWAY SWEDEN FINLAND

UNITED KINGDOM
DENMARK

IRELAND

NETH. E.
BEL. W.
GER. GER. POLAND

EUROPE

ASIA

UNION OF SOVIET SOCIALIST REPUBLICS

FRANCE

SWITZ.
LUX.
AUS. HUN. ROMANIA
CZECH.

MONGOLIA

PORTUGAL SPAIN

MONACO
ANDORRA

ITALY
SAN
MARINO

YUGO. BUL.
ALB.
GREECE

CHINA

N. KOR. JAPAN

TURKEY

S. KOR.

MOROCCO

TUNISIA

CYPRUS LEB.
MALTA

SYRIA IRAQ

ISR.

IRAN

AFGHANISTAN

MEDITERRANEAN SEA

JORDAN

PACIFIC

ALGERIA

LIBYA

EGYPT

KUWAIT

PAKISTAN

NEPAL

BHU.

TAIWAN

Tropic of Cancer

OCEAN

MAURITANIA

MALI

NIGER

CHAD

AFRICA

SUDAN

SAUDI
ARABIA

BAHRAIN QATAR

U.A.E.

OMAN

INDIA

BANGL.

MYANMAR

PHILIPPINE

SEA

SENEGAL

YEMEN
A.R.

P.D.R.
YEMEN

ARABIAN

THAILAND

CAMB.

VIETNAM

PHILIPPINES

GUI.
BIS.

GUINEA

BURKINA
FASO

DJI.

SEA

BRUNEI

SIERRA LEONE

IVORY
COAST

NIGERIA

C.A.R.

ETHIOPIA

SRI LANKA

MALAYSIA

LIBERIA

GHANA

CAMEROON

SOMALIA

MALDIVES

SINGAPORE

KIRIBATI

SÃO TOMÉ AND
PRINCIPE

TOGO

EQ.
GUI.

UGANDA

KENYA

Equator

NAURU

GABON

RWA.

SEYCHELLES

INDONESIA

PAPUA
NEW
GUINEA

SOLOMON
IS.

TUVALU

BU.

ZAIRE

TANZANIA

INDIAN

CORAL

VANUATU

FIJI

ANGOLA

ZAMBIA

MALAWI

COMOROS

OCEAN

SEA

MOZAMBIQUE

NAMIBIA

ZIMBABWE

MADAGASCAR

Tropic of Capricorn

BOTSWANA

MAURITIUS

AUSTRALIA

SWA.
LESO.

SOUTH
AFRICA

ATLANTIC

OCEAN

NEW
ZEALAND

Prime Meridian

Arctic Circle

Antarctic Circle

ANTARCTICA

Abbreviations

ALB.	—Albania	C.A.R.	—Central African Republic	LEB.	—Lebanon	RWA.	—Rwanda
AUS.	—Austria	CZECH.	—Czechoslovakia	LESO.	—Lesotho	S. KOR.	—South Korea
BANGL.	—Bangladesh	DJI.	—Djibouti	LIE.	—Liechtenstein	SWA.	—Swaziland
BEL.	—Belgium	E.GER.	—East Germany	LUX.	—Luxemburg	SWITZ.	—Switzerland
BHU.	—Bhutan	EQ. GUI.	—Equatorial Guinea	NETH.	—Netherlands	U.A.E.	—United Arab Emirates
BU.	—Burundi	GUI. BIS.	—Guinea Bissau	N. KOR.	—North Korea	W. GER.	—West Germany
BUL.	—Bulgaria	HUN.	—Hungary	P.D.R.–YEMEN	—People's Democratic	YEMEN A.R.	—Yemen Arab Republic
CAMB.	—Cambodia	ISR.	—Israel		Republic of Yemen	YUGO.	—Yugoslavia

Mini Facts

OFFICIAL NAME: Republic of Finland (in Finnish, Suomi)

LOCATION: Finland lies between 59°30'10" and 70°5'30" north latitude. Its westernmost point is 20°30'17" longitude, and easternmost is 31°35'20".
To the west it has a 335-mi. (586-km.) border with Sweden; to the north is the tip of Norway, with which it has a 453-mi. (716-km.) border; to the east is the Soviet Union, with a long 788-mi. (1,269-km.) border. Only China and Mongolia have longer borders with the Soviet Union.
To the south and southwest is the Baltic Sea, with its two arms, the Gulf of Finland, and the Gulf of Bothnia. The Baltic Sea is really a sea only in summer, since it is mostly frozen solid in winter. The Baltic has many rivers pouring into it, and the fresh water reduces the salt content and causes the sea to freeze very quickly in winter.

AREA: 130,558 sq. mi. (338,145 sq. km.), slightly larger than New Mexico. It is fifth in size of the Western European nations, but its population is small.

CAPITAL: Helsinki (in Swedish, Helsingfors)

POPULATION: 4,901,000 (1989 estimate)

MAJOR LANGUAGES: Finnish and Swedish

RELIGIONS: Evangelical Lutheran and The Orthodox Church in Finland

TYPE OF GOVERNMENT: Parliamentary democracy

HEAD OF STATE: President

HEAD OF GOVERNMENT: Prime Minister

PARLIAMENT: *Eduskunta* (in Swedish, *Riksdag*) or Parliament is a unicameral body of 200 representatives elected by direct vote every four years; it enacts laws and decides on the budget.

ADULT LITERACY: 99% (1989 estimate)

LIFE EXPECTANCY: Female, 78.0 years; male, 70.0 years

MAIN PRODUCTS: *Farming*—Dairy products, eggs; wheat and rye; cattle, potatoes, sugar beets; furs. *Forestry*—Birch, pine, spruce. *Manufacturing and Processing*—Wood and wood products, paper and pulp; metals; farm and industrial machinery; transportation equipment (including buses, ships, especially icebreakers); chemicals; textiles and clothing. *Mining*—copper, granite, limestone.

CURRENCY: *markka* (Finnmark)

Finland:
The Land of
Frost and Dreams

The novelist Johannes Linnankoski (1869–1913) said of his native
Finland:

> *This is a land with frost in the ground,*
> *These are people with dreams.*

Finland lies close to the shores of the Arctic Ocean, on the very edge
of Europe; it is a cold but fascinating land whose long winter season
shapes the rest of the year. Nature places many restrictions on cultivation, but the Finns have continually created new ways to adapt and—in
spite of recent urbanization and industrialization—Finns still live closer
to nature than most Europeans. Finland contains some of the last
wilderness areas in Europe, and even in the cities one is never far from
the forest.

In the past Finns had to struggle against nature and against foreign intruders. There were losses along the way, but the struggle gave them great strength. The early settlers found inspiration in the Finnish landscape and sky and in mythological heroes who taught them that it was possible to overcome obstacles. In more recent times the same sources have inspired the artists, musicians, and architects who have made Finland known to the world.

The Finns have had to start over from scratch so often that they have developed *sisu*: a special strength and stubborn determination not to give up in the face of adversity. The Finns define it as an almost magical quality, a combination of stamina, courage, and obstinacy held in reserve for times of emergency. In the darkest days of World War II, Finnish soldiers put the word *sisu* on their tanks.

Despite over seven hundred years of rule, first by Swedes and then by Russians, and the presence of a major superpower (the U.S.S.R.) along its border, the Finns have never given up their dream of independence and security. After fighting too many heroic but losing battles, they know that their freedom is best maintained through peace in the world. Finland is active as a leader of neutral nations and as peace observers in troubled lands.

Today Finland is a prosperous industrial nation. This seems to surprise and embarrass some Finns, for only "yesterday" they were eating bread made from pine bark. Some Finns think the need for *sisu* has passed, and yet they still seem willing to take a risk when it is called for—perhaps more often now on the ski slope or in a car rally or in an innovative design.

The Finns also have a reputation for caution and reserve. A Finnish proverb states that "silence is a person's best friend, for it remains behind after the rest has gone." Bertolt Brecht, the German playwright, who was a refugee in Finland in 1940, jokingly remarked that a Finn is "someone who says nothing in two languages (Finnish and Swedish)."

The Finns' closeness to nature is expressed in their mythology and in their feelings for birds and forests. This man says he can communicate with the birds. The photographer believes him. Tuula Huotelin-Meyer

Yet the Finns can be staunch friends, and their reserve is lessening as more and more of them are becoming city dwellers and world travelers. Even the formality of the Finnish language is changing, and patterns of speech are becoming much more colloquial.

Finland has developed rapidly in the last fifty years. Today all Finns learn several foreign languages in school, and the differences between classes and regions within the country are decreasing, as are the differences between Finland and the rest of the Western world.

Although most Finns now live in modern comfort, they have not abandoned their original values. They always return to the forest cabin to be alone with nature. The roots are still there: the forest, the water, the cabin, the sauna, and the silence.

FINLAND

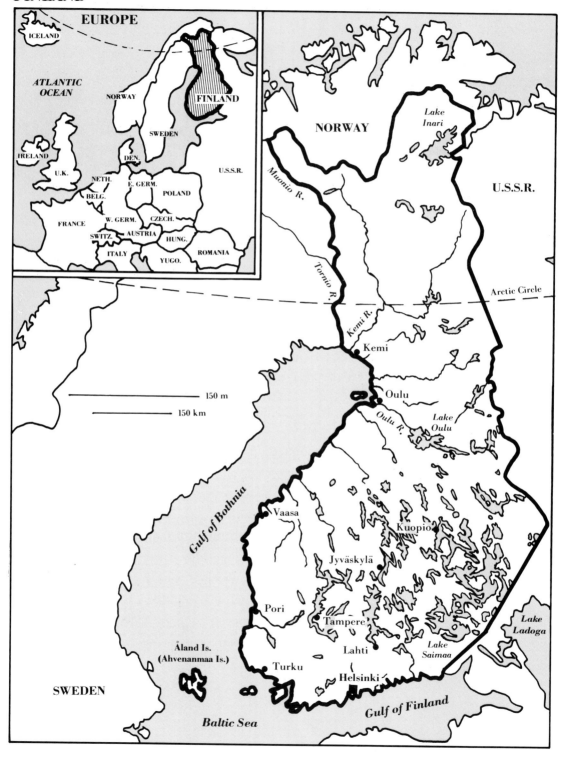

EUROPE

ICELAND

ATLANTIC
OCEAN

NORWAY

SWEDEN

FINLAND

IRELAND

U.K.

DEN.

U.S.S.R.

NETH.

E. GERM.

BELG.

POLAND

W. GERM.

CZECH.

FRANCE

SWITZ.

AUSTRIA

HUNG.

ITALY

YUGO.

ROMANIA

NORWAY

Lake
Inari

U.S.S.R.

Muonio R.

Tornio R.

Arctic Circle

Kemi R.

Kemi

Oulu

Oulu R.

Lake
Oulu

150 m

150 km

Gulf of Bothnia

Vaasa

Kuopio

Jyväskylä

Pori

Tampere

Lahti

Lake
Saimaa

Lake
Ladoga

Åland Is.
(Ahvenanmaa Is.)

Turku

Helsinki

SWEDEN

Baltic Sea

Gulf of Finland

The Northern Setting

Finland (*Suomi*) stands at the extreme north of the inhabited world. About one quarter of Finland's area lies above the Arctic Circle, making it and Iceland the northernmost independent countries in the world. Finland's neighbors are Sweden, Norway, and the Soviet Union. Of all the people in the world who live north of the Circle, almost half live in Finland.

Despite its location, the climate is milder than in other places at the same northern latitude. Temperatures are moderated by the Gulf of Bothnia in the west, the numerous shallow inland lakes, and most importantly, the west winds warmed by the Gulf Stream. But Finland can experience Siberian winters, with temperatures falling to 30 and 40 degrees below zero (Fahrenheit *or* Centigrade) even in the south, as happened in 1939–1940 and occasionally in other years.

Finland is a fairly large country, a little larger than the state of New

(Above) Winter walks are often on frozen lakes. Occasionally a propeller-driven iceboat is used for faster transport across the ice. The background is the Kotka factory of Enzo-Gutzeit, Finland's largest wood-processing company.   Hannu Vanhanen

(Right) A child's sled, made of plastic or fiberglass, travels easily on city paths. It is called a pulkka *after the reindeer-pulled Arctic sleds. Finnish industrial artists are noted for their design of simple, effective sports equipment.*   Hannu Vanhanen

Mexico. All of this area is populated by fewer than 5 million people—far less than the population of New York City.

Because it is so far north, Finland was one of the last areas in Europe to be settled. Sixty-five percent of the land is still forest; ten percent is lakes and rivers.

Finns have made good use of their forests and waterways and have drawn an almost spiritual strength from their northern landscape.

Though there has been a major migration of people to the southern part of Finland since the 1950's, each winter many Finns ski cross-country through the forests and each summer they head for the countryside to commune with nature. By law, every Finn is guaranteed the right of access to the countryside. Anybody can walk through the woods, swim in lakes, and pick berries for their own use as long as they do not disturb the peace of the owners or the reindeer.

Memories of the Last Ice Age

The landmass of Finland is still adjusting to the impact of the Ice Age that began about a million years ago. Only 12,000 years ago, when people began to plant crops in the Middle East, Finland was entirely buried under a continental ice sheet. When Central Europe was a treeless tundra and southern Europe a region of coniferous forests, ice covered the whole of Northern Europe. Finland began to emerge from the ice only after 10,000 B.C. and was completely free from it about 3,000 years later.

During the Ice Age the thick ice sheet pressed the crust of the earth down with its enormous weight, flattening much of the land into a plain or a basin. As the ice began to melt, the land started to rise, very quickly at first and then more gradually. The melted ice made a large sea, and only the east and north of Finland appeared above water.

Ice was decisive in forming the present face of Finland, carving hollows in the original bedrock, raising ridges, boulders, and cliffs from moraines. (A moraine is an accumulation of earth and stones carried and finally deposited by a glacier.) On top of the bare granite the retreating ice deposited its debris. The process was not a steady one. The ice sheet halted in its retreat at least three times. Small ridges may be found where the ice halted for only a winter. One set of moraine ridges, the grand Salpausselkä ridges, often referred to as the "backbone of Finland," is a zone where the border of the ice oscillated for several centuries, around 8,000 B.C., accumulating morainic layers and forming high ridges.

One of the most dramatic ridges is the tree-covered Punkaharju in the southeast, an extremely steep and narrow gravel ridge about five miles long that divides two large lake systems (Puruvesi and Pihlajavesi). Since 1877 the ridge has been designated an area for forestry research, and it is now also a natural reserve through which one can travel by car or train.

Finns consider Punkaharju one of their famous beauty spots. Retretti, Finland's newest art museum, is built entirely in the caves beneath the ridge. Finnish Ministry for Foreign Affairs/Press and Cultural Center

Rising from the Sea

A reminder of the glacial period is the fact that Finland is still emerging from the sea. The country's area grows by 2.7 square miles (7 square kilometers) a year, changing the contours of the coast and offshore islands and even the interior lakes. The greatest amount of land upheaval occurs along the Gulf of Bothnia on the west coast, where some towns have been forced to move their harbors out into deeper waters as the land rises.

The Finnish archipelago consists of thousands of islands that form a series of stepping stones across the Baltic Sea. Land that is an integral part of mainland Finland was previously part of this archipelago. Even now newer islands are appearing in the outer rim of this group of islands.

By the time the major upheavals of the Ice Age were over, there was only a thin covering of soil on top of the ancient bedrock. Most of Finland's bedrock is over 1.5 billion years old, making it some of the oldest in the world. Finland's flatness is also due to this very old and thoroughly weathered bedrock. Three quarters of the area of Finland lies on this foundation of granite, which breaks through the surface so often that granite has become the symbol for the whole country.

The thin soil on top of the bedrock is frequently deficient in nutrients. It is also often frozen and poorly drained. As a result, the Finns have had to work hard to make the land productive. Neither coal- nor oil-bearing rocks can be found in Finland, though there are deposits of copper, iron, and some other ores.

Northern Animals

Though the Ice Age destroyed all life in the territory of Finland, some animal species, such as the Norwegian lemming, were able to survive on ice-free refuges on the ocean coast. Most current animal species resemble those found in the northern parts of Scandinavia and the Soviet Union, and many are fairly recent arrivals that came from the south and east after the retreat of the glaciers. Animal migration is still going on. Recent arrivals are the mink and the flying squirrel, which has now practically disappeared from the rest of Europe. There are also wolves and lynx and bears that have crossed the eastern border into Finland.

The reindeer in the far north are descendants of the early wild reindeer that lived at the edge of the glacier about 10,000 years ago (8,000 B.C.). They helped to supply meat, skins, and bones that allowed early humans to live and adapt in spite of the cold.

The Saimaa seal, a rare freshwater seal, is a special relic of the Ice Age. Seals had lived in the Baltic Sea when it was a freshwater lake. As the land began to emerge from the Baltic, the Saimaa seal was separated from its old habitat and was "entrapped" in its own inland freshwater niche, where it has survived these many years, while the surrounding water has become a salty sea.

As recently as the turn of the century, the Saimaa seal was common in the Saimaa Lake System. Today it is considered the most endangered animal in Finland. Because of the damage it caused fishermen, a bounty used to be paid for shooting it. But in 1955, when it was almost too late, the Saimaa seal was officially protected. Now there are about 140 of them, and there are special areas where net fishing is prohibited because the young seals often drown in fishing nets. In recent years 85 percent of the seal pups have survived. The Saimaa seal has become one of the symbols of the conservation movement in Finland, reminding the Finns that they need to be in harmony with their natural setting in spite of the benefits of their rapid industrialization and urbanization.

Bears

The Finns chose the bear as their national animal in a referendum in the fall of 1985. Because of their close connection with the forest, this choice was not surprising. The bear is "the king of the forest" and has always played an important part in Finnish stories and folktales. A bear statue stands guard in front of the National Museum in Helsinki.

In the past, the bear was so feared that its name could not be spoken. Instead it was spoken of in euphemisms like *mesikämmen* (honey paw) and *metsän omena* (apple of the forest). These terms still exist in modern Finnish.

The title of *karhunkaataja* (bear hunter) carried great prestige, especially in earlier days. The killing of a bear was accompanied by a large celebration at which its meat was eaten and its spirit was calmed by songs. Many of the songs sung at these feasts can be found in Finland's national epic, the *Kalevala.* The final act honoring the bear was to return its skull and bones to the forest.

The Finnish bear is also a symbol of the forest. In spite of being feared, the bear was thought to be reliable and just. In Finnish folktales, the bear is usually depicted as gentle and clumsy and not too bright.

There are about four to six hundred bears in Finland today, and bear hunting is strictly regulated. Between forty and fifty bears are shot each year.

Most live in the eastern part near the border with the Soviet Union, but one can encounter bears anywhere in Finland. Some gourmet restaurants serve bear meat.

The Green Gold of the Forests

A Finnish proverb states that "Finland without forests would be like a bear without a skin." Finland is the most densely forested country in Europe, and the forests have been called Finland's "green gold." The export of plywood, paper, pulp, and cardboard has been the mainstay of the Finnish economy.

The hunting lodge of Marshal Mannerheim in Häme, with its large oven, planked floors, and exposed beams, reflects the search for the authentic Finnish style. Finnish Tourist Board

In the past forests supplied material for building homes and furniture, as well as boats, wagons and sleighs, plates, tankards, and all the implements of house and farm that can be fashioned out of wood. In addition, backpacks, shepherds' horns, and slippers were made out of birchbark. As early as 1638 Finnish settlers took their forestry skills to Delaware, where they introduced the log cabin to America.

Land of a Thousand Lakes

Finns are rarely far from water. In relation to its size Finland has more lakes than any other country in the world. The lakes are hard to count, since in Central and Eastern Finland—often called the Lake Plateau or Lake District—the lakes are connected by many streams and channels. Almost all are quite irregular.

Finnish lakes tend to be shallow and in some places turn to bogs, or marshes. This fact led to the idea that the Finnish word for Finland, Suomi, came from the stem *Suo-*, meaning marsh, and *maa-*, meaning land. However this interpretation is currently out of vogue with linguists, who are studying other possible explanations involving loan words and sound shifts. Scholars also stress that the lakes were once deeper than they are today.

In the past a church parish usually consisted of those families who lived around a lake. On summer Sundays one or two large parish rowboats would go from house to house picking up churchgoers, who would start singing the Lutheran hymns while rowing to church. The biggest church boats were 45 yards (41 meters) long, had eighteen pairs of oars, and could carry 150 people. On the return journey from church, the boats often raced, reaching speeds of up to seven knots.

In winter the parishioners crossed the frozen lakes by horse-drawn sleighs or on skis. Today buses travel over the frozen lakes, and car rallies and driving lessons are held on specially cleared ice tracks. The only difficult times are when the lakes are half frozen in early winter or half thawed in spring.

The Certainty of Winter

Because of the country's northern location, the one sure thing about the Finnish year is that winter is never far away. Finns speak of autumn winter, high winter, and spring winter. If the summer is particularly cold, it is called "green winter." As the Finnish writer Toivo Pekkanen (1902–1957) put it: "Winter is the only real season of the year. Spring is but a promise. . . . Summer is an illusion. . . . But winter is indeed of our essence: Snow, ice, and cold are a part of our nature. Winter never betrays us. Its arrival is a certainty."

At its strongest, winter smothers the entire country with snow and covers the Baltic Sea with ice so deep that fleets of icebreakers are needed to keep the harbors partially open. In the far north the snow may arrive in late September and be on the ground until May (averaging 210 days). Farther south it may not appear until December and may last only 110 days.

In the past, winter meant hardship, hunger, and illness. Modern technology and prosperity have changed that. Windows are double- and triple-glazed against the cold. Telephones, planes, helicopters, snowmobiles, and special tractor snow buses mean that even in the far north people are no longer so cut off and snowbound. The extra cost of winter to the Finnish people has been calculated to be about 4 to 8 percent of the national income. Finns have learned to live with winter, dressing in warm and often colorful designer-style outfits. They enjoy skiing, skating, sledding, ice fishing, and even car racing on frozen lakes.

It takes 22,000 horsepower to break the thick layer of Baltic ice, and Finland has a large fleet of ships to keep the lanes open in the winter. Finland is the world's leading manufacturer of icebreakers. Wärtsilä

The northern location creates a long winter, but it also brings a spectacular, though short, summer. The long dark nights of winter are then balanced by summer days almost twenty-four hours long, which allow many vegetables, berries, and fruits to ripen rapidly and children to play late into the night.

The sun disappears completely for much of December and January in the northernmost part of the country, though the nights are brightened by the reflection of the snow and occasional brilliant bursts of the northern lights (*aurora borealis*). The part of Finland within the Arctic Circle (above 66 ′30° N) is called the Land of the Midnight Sun, for the sun never sets from mid-May to mid-July. In other parts of the country, though the sun officially sets for two to four hours during the summer, there is still a great deal of light throughout the night.

The contrasts in the seasons are emphasized by the changing light of the subarctic. In all seasons the quality of light is special. Darkness in Finland is never so dark that it does not contain some gleam of light,

After boring a hole in the frozen lake with a special drill, the ice fisher may wait for hours before skiing or walking back to shelter. Contests bring out hundreds of enthusiasts for a modern sport that was once a means of survival. Finnish Tourist Board

and the light is never so bright that it does not hold some shadow. The eighteenth-century French geographer Maupertius traveled to Finland and marveled at the May sun in Lapland. "It was a remarkable picture," he said, "to see it shine so long on a horizon of ice; to see summer in the heavens while it was still winter on earth."

The midnight sun over Lake Pallasjärvi north of the Arctic Circle, photographed each hour for five hours and at the same level of the horizon. Finnish Tourist Board

GEOGRAPHIC REGIONS OF FINLAND

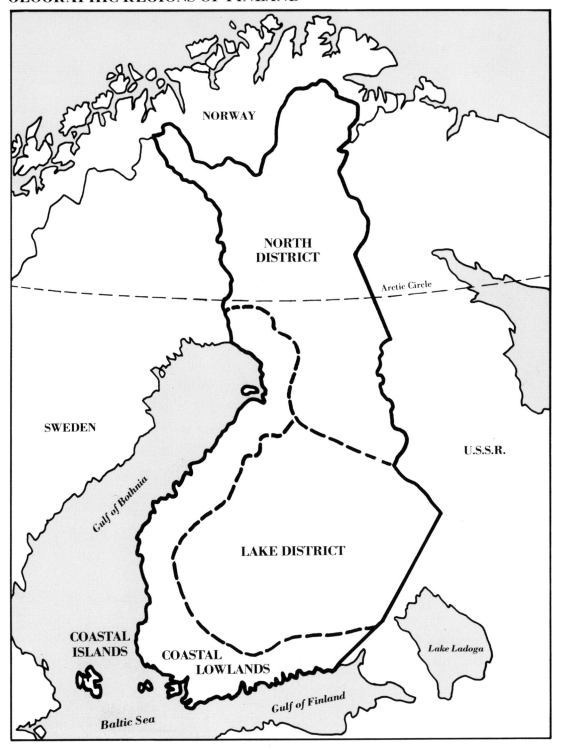

NORWAY

NORTH
DISTRICT

Arctic Circle

SWEDEN

Gulf of Bothnia

U.S.S.R.

LAKE DISTRICT

COASTAL
ISLANDS

COASTAL
LOWLANDS

Lake Ladoga

Baltic Sea

Gulf of Finland

The People of Finland

Finland, with 4.9 million inhabitants, is one of the most sparsely populated countries in Europe. Its history, drawing on influences from East and West, has given the people of Finland a special perspective. The great majority of Finns are Finnish speakers (93.6 percent), but there are also Swedish speakers, Lapps, Gypsies, and Karelians, each with a unique history and outlook.

Finnish Speakers

Finns like to think they have a special background that is a little more exotic, or wilder, than that of the sober Swedes. They do have a unique place among the peoples of northern Europe because they speak a language that is very different from the mother tongues of their Swedish, Norwegian, or Russian neighbors. Finnish is not an Indo-European

Whatever the topic, Finnish speakers always have at least three ways to say it. Hannu
Vanhanen

language but is related to other Balto-Finnic tongues such as Estonian,
Livonian, and Veps.

Years ago the Finns were described as descendants of people who
traveled west from a region in Siberia, settled south of the Baltic (in
present day Estonia), and then, described as the "Baltic Finns," arrived
in Finland sometime between 400 B.C. and 200 A.D.. This theory, based
on similarities in language, is no longer accepted by scholars, but it
stimulated many popular debates about a Finnish Asian past.

Scholars currently have a different picture, though it is not complete.
The Finns are probably descended from both the original population
that moved into the southern part of the country from the east after the
last Ice Age (around 7,200 B.C.) and peoples who came in a whole series

The Finnish Language

Finnish identity is closely associated with the Finnish language. Though Finland is part of Europe, Finnish is not related to any of the major European languages. It belongs to the Balto-Finnic branch of the Finno-Ugric language family. Thus its origins are completely different from those of English, for example, which belongs to the Germanic branch of the Indo-European language family.

Finnish is related to Estonian, Karelian, Veps, Votic, and Livonian, which are spoken south and east of Finland. Finns and Estonians watch each others' television programs across the Baltic and feel ties of kinship through their language.

Sami (formerly called Lappish) is distantly related, and it is not easy for Finns to understand. Hungarian is more distantly related to Finnish, the resemblances being chiefly structural, though the two languages do possess a small stock of ancient words in common. Some linguists suspect a link between Uralic and Altaic languages (including Turkish and Korean), although the evidence is not strong.

Finnish, Estonian, and Hungarian are official national languages. Aside from Sami, the other Finno-Ugric tongues are spoken by small groups scattered throughout the Soviet Union.

Finnish has borrowed vocabulary from various Indo-European languages over the course of the centuries, particularly from Swedish: Finnish *kakku* is the Swedish *kaka,* which is the English *cake.* Aside from such loan words, Finnish vocabulary is difficult and strange sounding to foreigners, as can be seen in the following words:

polkupyörä: bicycle
kirjekuori: envelope
sanomalehti: newspaper
kylpyhuone: bathroom

Some features of the language are:

1. Finnish uses many vowels and few consonants. The many vowels account for the pleasing sound of Finnish. The length of the sounds makes a difference in meaning, however. For example, *tuli* means "fire," *tuuli* means "wind," and *tulli* means "customs."

2. Finnish does not distinguish feminine, masculine, or neuter in pronouns or nouns, as many languages do. Thus, *Han puhuu suomea* states, "The human [as opposed to nonhuman] speaks Finnish." It could mean "She speaks Finnish" or "He speaks Finnish." Finnish may be more egalitarian than English in that the speaker does not focus on the issue of gender. When it is important, the speaker can always say: *Nainen puhuu suomea* ("The woman speaks Finnish") or *Mies puhuu suomea* ("The man speaks Finnish").

3. Words are formed by adding endings to the stem. Finnish does not have separate articles, prepositions, and pronouns. These are indicated at the end of the word: *lla* means "on" (*katolla*: "on the roof"), *lta* means "off" (*katolta*: "off the roof"), and *lle* indicates "onto" (*katolle*: "onto the roof"). There are 15 such endings in Finnish, with elaborate rules governing their use!

The Finnish language also builds new nouns and verbs from the basic stem of a word. Thus:

kirja = book
kirja + *sto* = library
kirjasto + *sta* + *mme* = out of our library
kirjo + *ita* + *n* + *ko?* = shall I write?

4. Finnish has a relatively free word order. Compare this Finnish sentence with English:

Englannin kielen harrastaminen on Suomessa hyvin yleistä.

Translated literally, that sentence would read "English language, the practice of is Finland-in very common." Actually, the sentence means "The practice of English is very common in Finland." If one wanted to stress "in Finland," that would be the first word in the sentence: *Suomessa englannin kielen harrastaminen on hyvin yleistä.*

A characteristic feature of Finnish speech is what has been called its "indirectness." The question "Would you like some coffee?" is usually phrased as "May there be coffee?" (*Saako olla kahvia?*) If the answer to a request is "no," the refusal might be quite roundabout. The question "Could you give me a haircut this afternoon?" might be answered, "It doesn't appear likely to fit" (*Ei se nyt taida sopia*).

Until recently, there were three levels of formality, or three ways to address someone. The most formal required using titles and special forms of the verb and pronoun: "Mr. Harbor Master, Sir, what would you buy?" The second, quite unusual in English, was to address someone in the third person: "What would the man buy?" Finally, among close friends, a first name and the informal pronoun could be used: "What will you buy (Hannu)?" Today, there is little use of the most formal mode of address, though the indirect third person is still common.

Even counting Finns living abroad, fewer people speak Finnish than live in New York City. More and more Finns learn English and other foreign languages to communicate beyond their borders. But still, as individuals and as a nation, the *aidinkieli* ("mother tongue") is a precious possession.

of migrations from the east, south, and west at different times over 10,000 years.

Once, most of Russia was inhabited by peoples speaking Finnish or languages related to it. They were pushed west by invading Slavs; so some of the Finns' ancestors came from the European part of Russia. But Scandinavians also traveled east to Finland in prehistoric as well as historic times, and people crossed the Baltic from the south first to hunt and then to settle. The Finnish population reflects all these migrations over many centuries.

Today the Finns consider themselves European, but they hold on to their non-Indo-European language with tremendous tenacity and affection. They have worked hard to preserve their linguistic and folkloric past.

Finland Swedes

Six percent of the population of Finland (just under 300,000) are Swedish speakers who trace their ancestry to the colonists who came to Finland between the twelfth and nineteenth centuries. They are small farmers and fishermen, important businessmen, diplomats, artists, and writers. For hundreds of years the Finland Swedes have lived along the coasts of west and southwest Finland.

Swedish speakers held a dominant position in the past when Finnish was not even allowed to be taught in the schools. Until the mid-nineteenth century, Swedish was the official language of the country, and there were bitter divisions between the two language groups. Since World War II, the language controversy has been pushed into the background. The task of rebuilding the country made these rivalries seem trivial.

Today Finland is officially a bilingual nation. The country's two languages are Finnish and Swedish. The rights of the Finland-Swedish minority are safeguarded in the Constitution. Special provisions guarantee equality in the church, the defense forces, and civil service. Speakers of either language can request services in their "mother tongue," and applicants for any but the lowest-level jobs must be bilingual.

Much time is spent on languages in Finnish schools. Swedish is taught in Finnish-language schools, just as Finnish is now taught in Swedish-language schools. But English has become more and more popular, and as Finnish-speaking students choose to study it rather than Swedish, the issue of language may again become a problem in the future.

The Swedish People's Party, which was founded in 1906 as a unifying party for Finland Swedes, receives 72 percent of the Finland-Swedish vote and regularly elects representatives to Parliament. Finland Swedes continue to send their children to Swedish schools and support a whole range of cultural organizations: the Swedish Theater in Helsinki; a Swedish-speaking university in Turku, Åbo Academy; numerous Swedish-language newspapers, and Swedish-language television and radio broadcasts.

While they have many of their historical roots in Sweden, the Finland Swedes have always considered themselves citizens of Finland. Given the country's close involvement in Nordic cooperation, Swedish speakers will continue to be an important link between Finland and its Nordic neighbors.

Sami (Lapps)

The Sami are descendants of the original population that moved into Scandinavia from the east after the last Ice Age and now live in the north of Norway, Sweden, and Finland, and in the Kola peninsula in the U.S.S.R. They prefer to be called Sami rather than Lapps, for in their own language the word *sami* means "banished." In Norway, Sweden, and Russia, as well as in Finland, they were pushed out of the more fertile south farther and farther into the north. There they survived by hunting bears and wild reindeer, trapping beaver and other small animals, and fishing. Many of their earlier practices, such as telling the future on a shaman's drum, were abandoned or hidden when missionaries and government officials labeled them "heathen."

There are 4,000 Sami in Finland. They are vastly outnumbered by the Finns even in the northern province of Lapland—a few thousand Sami to about 200,000 Finns. Only in the northernmost corner of

Tourism has become an important industry in the far north. Sami dress in native costumes and take visitors on "reindeer safaris."   Finnish Tourist Board

The Shaman's Drum

The original Sami religion was based on animism (a belief that all natural objects and living beings have souls or spirits) and shamanism (a belief in the power of a religious mediator). These beliefs are found among most peoples who live near the North Pole.

The Sami shaman (*noaide*) was a man skilled in communicating with the supernatural. He had the assistance of a magical drum. All family heads used these drums, but the shaman was considered most effective because he could go into trance.

While playing the drums, his soul would travel, with the aid of a helper, to the underworld where spirits could help him to cure illness, make predictions, and avert disasters.

The skin of the drum had many stick-figure drawings. To predict the future, a small stick was placed on the head of the drum and the drum was shaken. The path that the stick took and where it stopped was carefully "read" to reveal messages from the spirit world.

Finland—in the rural districts of Enontekiö, Inari, Utsjoki, and Sodan-kylä—are they a majority.

Fewer than one in ten Sami are reindeer herders today, but many Sami traditions are linked with nature and the reindeer. Reindeer have to be lassoed and counted at roundups during the winter and in the summer, when some are slaughtered for meat and the young ones have their ears notched with their owners' identification marks. Among the Skolt Sami in eastern Finland, a child was given its first reindeer, called "first-tooth reindeer," when its first tooth came through. There are more than twenty different words for reindeer in the Sami language—a large reindeer, a bull, a calf, and so on—showing how important reindeer were to the Sami. Years ago the Sami hunted wild reindeer on skis and shot them down with bows and arrows only when they were needed for food. When the government asked that taxes be paid in skins, more deer had to be killed, and some Sami then became migratory herders, following the reindeer in an annual migration. Every year more and more Sami find jobs in the villages and small towns in the north and so fewer of them are herding reindeer.

At home the Sami speak a dialect of the ancient Sami language, a Finno-Ugric language distantly related to Finnish. At school the children learn to speak Finnish, since they are citizens of Finland, though a few northern schools have some instruction in Sami. Many Sami are trilingual, speaking Sami, Finnish, and Swedish or Norwegian. In the past those on the eastern border knew some Russian. Sami traders developed a language combining Norwegian, Russian, and Sami that they used in bartering meat and hides for Russian grain and wares.

Since World War II there has been a revival of Sami pride in their native traditions and an attempt to document and preserve their language, customs, and crafts, helped by the Sami Institute in Kautokeino, Norway. Nils Aslak Valkeapää, a musician, poet, and artist, was one of the founders of the World Council of Indigenous Peoples and is active as a spokesperson for his people. His book *Greetings from Finland: The Sami—Europe's Forgotten People*, published in 1986, is only the second book by a Sami author ever to appear in English.

The most recent threat to Sami existence came when the Chernobyl nuclear accident in April 1986 contaminated the reindeer's food supply, and thus the Sami's major source of meat. It will be many years before the full impact of this disaster is clear, but in spite of the changes the Sami may undergo, their story and how they adapted to the cold wilderness will not be forgotten.

Snowmobiles

Snowmobiles came to Finland in early 1962 and revolutionized the time required for travel. One group of Sami who had taken three days to travel by sled to a store in Norway could now make the trip in five hours.

But the snowmobile also made the Sami more dependent on the outside world. To buy the snowmobiles and gasoline required cash. Soon the snowmobiles created major differences of wealth among the Sami and changed their patterns of herding. The noise of the machine made the reindeer nervous and lowered their fertility rate. Some Sami wish they could return to the pre-snowmobile days.

Grass Socks in Winter

Nowadays the traditional Sami dress is fast disappearing except at Easter and weddings—and for footwear during winter. Many Sami swear that their boots and grass socks are better than any synthetic "moon boots" yet made.

The pointed-toed fur boot (*nutukas*) is made out of the hide of the reindeer's leg and decorated with colored cloth. Hay is placed inside the boot for additional warmth. The hay comes from a special sedge grass (*Carex lapponum*) that is gathered in the autumn, made pliable, and woven into plaits for storing.

The hay keeps the feet warm in hard frost or wet autumn weather. When the hay becomes damp, it may be rapidly dried in the heat of a fire. A reindeer herder goes through some fifty sets of "boot-grass" fillers in a year. In severe frost hay is added to gloves.

Finnish Gypsies

The Finnish Gypsies are the largest minority in Finland. The word *Gypsy* comes from *Egyptian*, but most scholars consider the Gypsies a dark Caucasoid people who originally migrated from India to Europe in the fourteenth or fifteenth century. They arrived in Finland during the sixteenth century, and more came in the seventeenth and eighteenth centuries when Swedish authorities drove them from Sweden proper and into the eastern half of Finland.

Unlike the Sami, who now wear their traditional costumes only at weddings and special occasions, the Finnish Gypsies have kept their native costumes. The women dress in long velvet skirts with many petticoats and elaborate aprons, blouses, and vests. The men wear long, dark suits.

Although they have been in Finland for centuries, their "different-ness" from ordinary Finns is striking, and they are often treated with suspicion. On occasion Gypsies have been barred from restaurants because they did not meet the dress code. They have faced discrimination in jobs and housing, and harrassment by the police. Although it was a fate the Gypsies feared, no Finnish Gypsies were turned over to the Germans or the Soviets in World War II.

The Gypsies formed the Finnish Gypsy Association in 1967 and got two important laws on the statute books: one prohibiting discrimination based on racial or ethnic origin (1970) and another aimed at improving their housing conditions (1975).

In the past the Gypsies were itinerant tinkers in the rural parts of Finland, particularly in the north and east. They lived in horse-drawn carts and made their living repairing metal objects, trading horses, selling handicrafts, and telling fortunes. Though relationships were sometimes tense, Gypsy families had ties with local farmers who gave

them food and shelter in exchange for horses and labor, especially during the summer harvest.

After World War II the situation of the Gypsies in the countryside changed. Tractors replaced horses, metal objects gave way to plastics, and newspaper horoscopes made fortune-telling obsolete. In the 1960's many Gypsies moved to the cities, often into the poorest areas, especially in the south. Nearly a quarter of the Gypsy population left for Sweden as social refugees, hoping for better social services. Some continued to sell lace or turned to selling alcohol. Occasionally Gypsy men get work as unskilled laborers, but the majority today are on welfare.

For centuries the Gypsies maintained their own distinct customs. The Finns view the Gypsies and their unwillingness to imitate Finnish ways as a "social problem," a euphemism used to describe situations about which they do not want to talk.

A few other groups, such as Jews and Turks, came through Russia as merchants in the late nineteenth century and remained. Most live in Helsinki, which has a synagogue and a mosque.

Karelians

Were it not for the Finnish–Soviet border, the Karelians would not be a separate people. They are eastern Finns, descendants of those who settled in the area from Lake Saimaa and Lake Ladoga (Ladozhskoye Ozero, in Russian) to Lake Onega around 5,000 B.C. and then spread

There are approximately 6,000 Gypsies in Finland, more than in any other Nordic country. The Finnish Gypsies call themselves "Romany" and speak a mixture of Romany and Finnish. Tuula Huotelin-Meyer

The Orthodox Church of Finland

The Orthodox Church of Finland was established in 1175 with the founding of the Valamo monastery on an island in Lake Ladoga. The monastery was relocated to Heinävesi in Finland's Lake District after World War II.

Karelian homes include an icon in the corner directly opposite the oven. It is called the "big corner" or "God's corner." According to tradition, a visitor should bow to this corner before greeting the host.

Services used to be held in Church Slavonic, and many priests were Russians. Just before Finnish independence (December 6, 1917), the Finnish Orthodox Congregation split away from the diocese in St. Petersburg and services were performed in Finnish. The Finnish Orthodox Church was declared autonomous in 1918, but in 1923 it was placed under the Ecumenical Patriarchate of Constantinople. There are now attempts to make the Finnish Church autonomous again.

Every village with an Orthodox prayer house traditionally holds an annual festival called a praasniekka *(from the Russian word* prazdnik*) in honor of a particular saint associated with the congregation.* Finnish Tourist Board

north to the White Sea and northwest to the Gulf of Bothnia. The border between Finland and Russia changed many times over the centuries and divided the Karelians into Western (Finnish) Karelians and Eastern (Russian) Karelians. At the end of World War II a large part of Finnish Karelia was ceded to the Soviets. Today Finnish Northern Karelia is a

province, with its capital at Joensuu, while the Soviet Karelian Autonomous Republic has its capital at Petroskoi.

Living close to and sometimes within Russia, the Karelians developed different traditions from those of the western Finns. They belong to the Eastern Orthodox Church with its double crosses, incense, icon paintings, and elaborate vestments—a sharp contrast to the simplicity of the Protestant Finnish Lutheran Church. The style of their architecture, and their diet and language, are also somewhat different.

Many parts of Karelia were far removed from cities and had few or no roads at all. The pace of change was slow. It is not surprising, then, that when, in the nineteenth century, Finnish scholars set out to find the "authentic Finnish" customs, they traveled through the backwoods of Karelia collecting folktales and copying down the decorative styles of the embroidery and wood carvings.

Karelia also included Viipuri (now Vyborg, in the Soviet Union), a lively and sophisticated cosmopolitan center, then Finland's second largest city. Tears come to the eyes of older Karelians when they describe the beautiful lakes and forests of their particular parish and tell how Russians now live in Viipuri.

All but a handful of the 430,000 Karelians living in lands ceded to the Soviet Union at the end of World War II picked up a few belongings, put them in carts, and walked, with their cattle, west into Finnish territory.

The Karelians were considered *suku* (kin), but the Finns' generosity in resettling the huge number of refugees—Karelians represented 12 percent of Finland's population—was an example to the world. The Karelians were relocated quickly and smoothly. Within seven years, all had been given homes and a means of livelihood.

Though they may have great nostalgia for their old homeland, the Karelians know they can never return and have adjusted to their place in modern Finland. They know their grandchildren may be Lutheran or Orthodox and will probably speak a more standard Finnish, but they hope that the history of Karelia will be preserved.

POPULATION DENSITY OF FINLAND

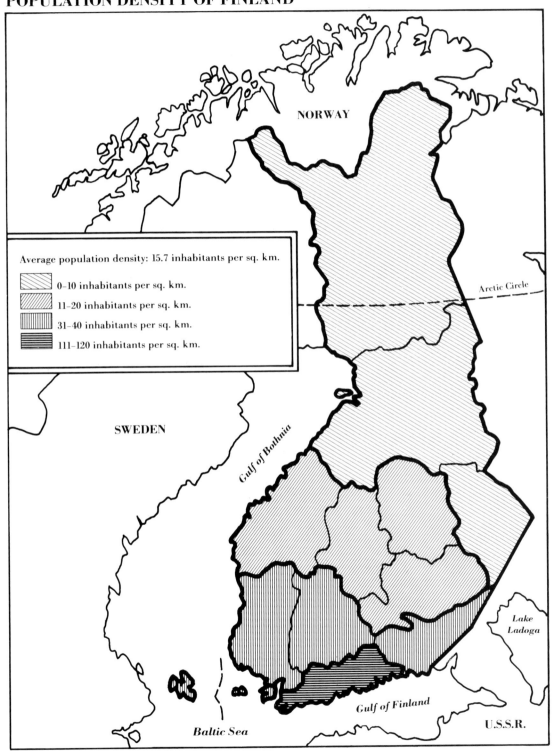

Average population density: 15.7 inhabitants per sq. km.

- 0–10 inhabitants per sq. km.
- 11–20 inhabitants per sq. km.
- 31–40 inhabitants per sq. km.
- 111–120 inhabitants per sq. km.

NORWAY

Arctic Circle

SWEDEN

Gulf of Bothnia

Gulf of Finland

Lake Ladoga

U.S.S.R.

Baltic Sea

The North Country

The north of Finland contains Europe's largest continuous wilderness. Here a hiker may range for days on end without meeting another person. Rock paintings along the Arctic Ocean and other excavated Stone Age sites just north of Finland's current border show that people lived in this region at least 8,000 years ago. But in historical times the north was settled last. In 1542 Gustavus Vasa, King of Sweden-Finland, declared that all land not privately owned henceforth belonged to the Crown. As a result, much of the northern third of Finland belongs to the state. Some of this forest land has recently been harvested and replanted. Other large sections are national wilderness parks.

Over 40 percent of Finland's land area can be described as northern. The Arctic Circle runs through Lapland near Rovaniemi, and the Sami live in the northernmost corner. The umbrella name for the vast provinces of northern Finland, Sweden, and Norway is *nordkalotten* in Swedish or *pohjoiskalotti* in Finnish.

The north is sometimes called Grassland (*nurmi*) Finland or Nature (*luonnon*) Finland, as opposed to the south, called Grain (*vilja*) Finland or Congested (*ruuhka*) Finland. This contrast reflects the fact that the north has far fewer inhabitants and a much shorter growing season than the south. Less than 2.5 percent of the area north of latitude 65° is cultivated. Leafy turnips and cereal grass for cattle fodder, as well as potatoes, can be grown because of the long summer daylight, but yields of rye, barley, and oats are meager. Pioneer farmers in the mid-eighteenth century often mixed the bark of trees with grain when making bread so as not to use up all the grain.

Nowadays most people have given up farming altogether, leaving only a few dairy farmers. The land is better suited for reindeer herding, fox and mink farming, fishing, and forestry. Tourism has also become an important part of the economy. The population density has risen, with 2.2 inhabitants per square kilometer in the province of Lapland and 7.6 in the province of Oulu, the two northernmost provinces. This is similar to the density of the state of Nevada, which is 7.3.

The North Country reminds the modern-day Finn of the hard demands nature made on all Finns in the past. There is a history of pioneer ventures here: the Sami herding reindeer; Finnish farmers carving out the wilderness to extend the unmarked border separating Finland from Russia; gold panners in the late 1800's hoping to get rich; the rebuilding of the countryside after the Germans burned everything in their path on retreating in 1944.

Today the wilderness has become quite "civilized" with helicopters, snowmobiles, and well-winterized cabins. Ski lifts swing up slopes of hills that were once largely the preserve of reindeer and grouse. But it has not been so long since the old Lapp saying "The Lapp is born to suffer as the bird is born to fly" was all too realistic. *Sisu*, that special strength required in difficult situations, was continually needed in the North Country.

The Oldest Part of Finland

The north region contains the geologically oldest parts of the country. Finland is basically a low-lying country, and only in the north does the land rise above a thousand feet. The highest mountains are in the northwest corner, where they merge with the mountain regions of Norway. Halti, Finland's highest point, is 4,370 feet (1,344 meters) above sea level. Here there is a definite feeling of the real Arctic, with no forests to be seen anywhere. Arctic fogs often cover Halti, whose flanks are snow-covered all year round.

The north is a land of large and small lakes, marshes, and great rivers. Lapland has Finland's longest rivers. The Kemi and the Tornio empty into the northern Gulf of Bothnia, but other rivers drain to the Arctic Ocean and still others into Russia. Salmon and whitefish once formed part of the everyday diet of those living beside these great rivers. The main thoroughfare of Lapland, the Kemi River, was closed off as a route for fish migration in 1948 when a hydroelectric power station was built at its mouth; but the Tornio River, which forms the border between Sweden and Finland, remains unharnessed. Whitefish are still caught in the traditional way with hoop nets at the rapids of Kukkolankoski, where huge quantities are smoked and served at an annual Whitefish Fair. Each summer this quiet area is briefly invaded by tourists and Finns who participate in the longest canoe race in the world.

The Finnish forests stretch surprisingly far north, ending with bare "fells" (hills) covered only with arctic shrub, mosses, and lichens. Finland has only a narrow band of tundra, where permafrost prevents any extensive growth. South of the tundra, peat bogs, called *taiga*, cover more than half the land area. These bogs are home to many birds, especially waders and waterfowl, including swans that migrate every spring and fall.

Whether using a home-made rod or the latest industrial design, Finns enjoy fishing in idyllic spots away from the crowd.   Tuula Huotelin-Meyer

Recently an extensive stretch of 10,000 acres (4,000 hectares) of the Keso peatlands in the northeast, which are over 9,000 years old, was made into a nature preserve. Several dozen bird species, some of which are very rare or almost extinct, nest in these peatlands. Local residents may go into the sanctuary only for a few weeks in the late summer to pick berries and mushrooms. Even photographers, for whom tall towers outside the preserve have been built, are barred.

Though the northern ecosystems support only a restricted range of animal and plant species, those that do thrive are represented in vast quantities. Thus there are huge numbers of bilberries, lingonberries, crowberries, forest mosses, reindeer lichen, mushrooms, mosquitoes, sand flies, reindeer, and willow grouse, but fewer reptiles, frogs, earthworms, or herbs.

"Winter Comes on the Wings of Swans"

The difference between the northern Nature Finland and southern Congested Finland is reflected in the views Finns have of the raven. A northern Finn looks at the raven and thinks of a scavenger. Southern Finns, on the other hand, regard it as the noble overseer of the wilderness depicted in Finnish romantic literature.

The Finns call the Milky Way "The Path of Birds." The Sami have a female spirit that protects migrating birds, and a "Land of Birds." The Land of Birds beyond "the edge of the sky" is one of the most ancient ideas in the mythology of Sami, Finns, and related peoples such as Estonians and Hungarians.

Most birds migrate to warmer areas, but a few, including the dipper, spend the winter in the north. It is the only bird that is more numerous in winter than in summer in Kuusamo, in northeast Finland. The dipper can dive into the coldest water, swimming like a seal and picking food out from a crevice between stones even in the depth of winter. It is the guardian of the last unfrozen spot, often near rapids. Long cold spells lessen even the dippers' chance of survival.

Snow falls almost every year in June, and stories are told of times when snow has fallen in every month of the year. The first spring arrivals, such as the swans, do not panic at a winter backlash in June. But they do leave with the first snowfall of winter, fulfilling an old Finnish saying that "winter comes on the wings of swans."

The Northern Winter   While snow does not accumulate to any great depth, the snowfall lasts at least half a year. Many trees look snow laden in the winter, but the covering is mainly ice and hoarfrost, layered on top of snow. The layering can continue all winter until the thick coating weighs more than 6,000 pounds (3,000 kilos) per tree, sometimes too much for the branches to withstand. On the fells of Lapland, between the forest and the tundra, blizzards tear at the trees, and though the short Lapland spruce and bushlike mountain birch can stand up to both the wind and the snow, they frequently lose their tops because of the weight of the ice and then fork in an odd manner, making them look like strange works of modern abstract sculpture.

Survival   The northern winter, with its "snow-forest climate," is a study in survival. Birds and animals must balance between searching for food and expending energy. Ruffled feathers protect a bird from the biting cold, but a resting spot must be carefully chosen for shelter and a chance to catch the fleeting warmth of any moments of sun. When the temperature drops below −40° F (−40° C) birds congregate together or sometimes seek shelter for the night in holes in the snow.

The arctic hare grows a white fur coat for the winter that contains at least twice the number of hairs of its brown summer coat. The bears hibernate. The reindeer learn to shovel snow with their hooves and to uncover lichen, a spongelike evergreen without roots that absorbs nutrients from the air. When the snow becomes deeper and harder and the reindeer can no longer dig for lichen, they may have to turn to beard moss, the lichen that grows on the branches and trunks of trees.

Finns have adopted special customs to deal with the severe weather, such as keeping doors unlocked so that a passing stranger can always come in to get out of the cold.

First Sign of Spring: An Icicle

Winter lasts for more than half the year. Then comes the first sign of spring: not a particular crocus or bird, but an icicle. Only then, when it has been warm enough for melting to begin, can the world begin to

Reindeer

The reindeer's ancestors used to wander freely across the north of Scandinavia. The modern-day reindeer have adapted to the forest, but their hooves are still especially good for navigating in snow and in summer marshes. Today they live as half-tame beasts. More and more reindeer spend the winter in farm courtyards, where they are given fodder, or in forests, where hay is delivered to them by snowmobile.

The reindeer's life still consists of many crises. In the uncertain spring weather, many newly born reindeer calves die. During the migration to summer grazing lands they often have to swim across wide channels, and many drown. Automobiles are a danger, particularly since Lapland has 3,000 miles of roads and the reindeer like the mosquito-free highways. They even have to be driven from the airfields to prevent them from getting in the way of planes.

The radioactive fallout from the Chernobyl nuclear accident in April 1986 contaminated the reindeer and their main source of food, the spongelike lichen. Some reindeer had to be slaughtered prematurely and were fed to minks being bred for fur.

expect the short spring and summer. The last of the snow in Lapland usually melts in May, so late that many plants and animals emerge directly into summer, without experiencing the trials of the cool spring felt farther south. The flowers burst forth so quickly that to many it seems a miracle of nature.

Rounding up the reindeer takes several weeks. Calves born at the beginning of May are earmarked around Midsummer. Altogether some twenty-odd cuts and marks are used in earmarking. Each reindeer owner makes up his or her own combination. When herders want to give their first-born child a reindeer, they add one nick to their own mark, two for the second child, and so on. Finnish Ministry for Foreign Affairs

Colors of Autumn

Lapland is known for its skiing season in early spring and for the "midnight sun" in summer. Yet the most beautiful season is autumn, when the first frost transforms the landscape. The birch trees stand like yellow flames, while the ground is ablaze with red berries, brown mushrooms, and light-green moss. There is still light late into the evening, and the sunsets, which last much longer at this latitude, are magnificent, huge masses of color. The Lapps connect the brilliant colors of autumn with the colors of the *aurora borealis* or northern lights of winter and the coming of spring.

Sami Legend of the Northern Lights

A Sami legend explains that human beings are like the leaves that turn a beautiful yellow in the autumn because they are going to die. As death approaches, the souls of human beings turn brighter also. But while the leaves fall to the ground, the souls fly up to the sky. When the shadows of winter lie on the earth, the souls come and show themselves to the living to give them courage to wait for the return of the spring and the sun. They dance from one end of the sky to the other, giving much better light than the moon or the stars.

Scientists are much less eloquent but are still researching the conditions (static electricity and temperature) that produce these brilliant displays of color.

Dwarf birch and shrubs, similar to those that first grew on the borders of the ice sheet, can still be found in the Arctic. Finnish Ministry for Foreign Affairs

The Lake District

The Lake District is called the "heart of Finland." It lies in a large central plateau, and its lakes and forests, occasionally interrupted by farmlands or wood-processing plants, are the setting for the majority of Finland's rural districts and inland cities.

Finland's largest lake is Lake Saimaa in the east, with 443 sq. mi. (1,147 sq. km.). It combines with several other lakes to form the Greater Saimaa System of 1,690 sq. mi. (4,377 sq. km.). One can travel by steamboat nearly two hundred miles in the Saimaa Lake System from one end to the other.

In Central Finland the lakes cover an average of over twenty-five percent of the surface. There are wide tracts where more than half of the area is covered with water. The lakes, which tend to be shallow, are connected by streams and channels, forming an intricate network of waterways that has influenced the choice of where roads could be built and the locations of communities and mills.

Sauna

Ask any Finn what is especially Finnish and the answer will certainly include the language and the *sauna* (a type of steam bath in a wooden building). *Sauna* is an old Finnish word that translates as "bathhouse," but to a Finn it stands for much more. Traditionally the sauna was built even before the house. It was the most essential of the farm buildings and served as a home until the dwelling house was ready. Children were born in the sauna, the sick were cared for, and sometimes meat was cured or nets dried in the sauna.

In some old bathhouses, there was a "wolf hole," through which farmers kept watch at night for the wolves that might come prowling around and shot them if they got the chance.

In pre-Christian times the sauna was a place of worship of the dead, who were supposed to return gladly to so pleasant a place. Since fire was sacred, the fireplace and stones were looked upon as altars. The steam of the sauna was associated with the life spirit. Today it is still said: "In the sauna one must conduct oneself as one would in church." When one is ill: "If alcohol, tar, and the sauna can avail nothing, then there is no other cure."

The sauna is well suited to Finland's forests, which supply the fuel and building materials. The traditional sauna is a small wooden cabin set near a lake. It is lined inside with natural birch and contains several tiers of wooden benches and a stove piled with large, rounded stones. The stones are heated before the bathers enter. Cleansing comes primarily through perspiration. The sauna is drier than the Turkish bath, although some moisture can be added by splashing water on the stones.

Any Finn will tell you that the best sauna is found in the countryside, for the stones should be heated by a wood fire and the sauna situated so the bathers can look out onto an idyllic scene near a lake or river. If possible the sauna should face west or southwest so the rays of the setting sun stream in, giving a feeling of calm.

Even in the cities, the Finns try to place the sauna in pleasant surroundings, with adjoining shower and a room for resting paneled in light birch and windows facing a forest. Apartment buildings, hospitals, hotels, athletic centers, and factories always have large saunas that can be reserved for private use or used communally. An average-sized sauna may hold about eight people, though others are much smaller. Saturday evening is the traditional sauna time. In the past, during harvest season the sauna was heated every evening.

The offer of a sauna bath is part of Finnish hospitality. It is always warmed for guests who have come from afar. Many Finns invite their friends to have a sauna in the same way that people in other countries invite friends in for a meal or a drink. People sit in the sauna and relax or chat quietly, taking a rest and a swim every so often to cool down. The sauna ritual must never be rushed, and it may last for several hours. Afterward, one sits and meditates or socializes quietly.

Finnish businessmen regularly take their clients to the sauna, believing it is conducive to successful negotiations. The President has a large sauna in which important guests are sometimes entertained. On more than one occasion President Urho Kekkonen of Finland discussed important matters of state in the sauna with the Premier of the Soviet Union.

Whether at war, at the Olympics, or as immigrants abroad, the Finns have taken the sauna with them. During the Winter War the sauna was made in tents lined with leaves and was especially important for getting rid of bugs. Finnish athletes are convinced that the sauna brings back their strength better than sleep.

While the sauna has similarities with the perspiration baths of the Eskimos and some American Indians, Finns are convinced that theirs is the best combination of dry and damp air for good health and pleasure. The Friends of the Finnish Sauna report that there are 1.4 million saunas in Finland. Certainly each of Finland's 4.9 million inhabitants could fit into a sauna somewhere at the same time.

The principal phases of a sauna:
1. Heat the stones until they become red hot. The ideal air temperature is about 190–200°F (85°–90°C), though it may be as high as 280°F (140°C).
2. The sauna should stand and "ripen" to distribute the heat evenly.
3. Sit on the wooden benches and perspire.
4. Produce steam by throwing water on the stones.
5. Beat yourself with a *vihta* (whisk) made from fresh, green, small birch branches. This improves circulation. (A Finnish proverb states, "Sauna without a *vihta* is like food without salt." Tradition says the branches should be gathered at full moon in the beginning of July.)
6. Wash with soap and water. (Many saunas have a separate washing room).
5. Rinse.
6. Cool off. (This is when you might jump into a cool lake or, in the winter, roll in the snow!)
7. Dry.
8. Rest. Repeat as often as you like.

Long ago hunters followed the waterways up from the south. Animal pelts, especially the red squirrel's, were used as currency. The Finnish word for money, *raha*, originally meant pelt. The regional coat of arms of Savo, a province in the Lake District, is a drawn bow, reminding the present-day Finns of the importance of hunting in the past.

Early settlers also followed the paths of lakes or rivers as they moved into the countryside. By the thirteenth century the western part of the Lake District had stable agricultural communities. In the late fifteenth century, farmers from both the southwest and east established small homesteads even farther north into the woodlands. A farm would be placed on the shore of a lake or, in the eastern Lake District, on a hilltop.

The early settlers cleared the land through slash-and-burn techniques. The basic method was to cut down trees one year, to burn them the next, using the ash to fertilize the soil, and then to plant crops (rye, barley, oats or buckwheat, and turnips) amid the tree stumps for four to six years. When the crops declined, the plots were left to reforest for twenty to thirty years while the farmers worked a newly cleared plot. Natural meadows provided hay for cattle. Hunting and fishing supplemented farming. These early settlements were known as wilderness farms.

Today the Lake District has mill towns and small agricultural communities with dairy farms. There are also cities, including Tampere, Finland's second largest city, in the west and Imatra in the east. Both of these developed into large industrial centers around waterfalls used for power. Cities like Hämeenlinna, Mikkeli, Jyväskylä, Kuopio, Savonlinna, and Lappeenranta each have special histories as fortresses, school towns, or commercial centers.

People have fished in Finland's gulfs, lakes, and rivers for as long as there have been inhabitants. For some, though fewer each year,

This day's catch is muikku, *a small whitefish delicious on a summer grill or in* kala-kukko.   Hannu Vanhanen

fishing remains the main means of livelihood, while for others it is a supplement or, increasingly, a sport. Fish is more important than meat in the diet of many Finns. The provincial dish of Savo is *kalakukko* (*kala* means fish). A *kukko* is a meal baked into a round, domed loaf of bread. The outer shell of the *kalakukko* is made of rye dough, while the filling contains whitefish, perch, and salt pork. The *kukko* bakes so long that the bones of the fish melt. There is a large bakery in Kuopio that sells *kalakukot* daily in the central marketplace and ships them throughout the country.

Water Transport

The Saimaa Lake System was the major route for transporting goods from the interior of Finland to the coast until World War II. In the 1860's matches made in Kuopio could be sent all the way to Russia by steamboats through various branches of the lake system. At Savonlinna the water route continued on the Vuoksi River and through the Saimaa Canal all the way to Viipuri and the Gulf of Finland. From there it was

While guiding tourists through the Lake District, this boat captain wears her Finnish national costume.   Hannu Vanhanen

Counting Finland's Lakes

The Finns have often wondered just how many lakes there are in their "country of a thousand lakes." In 1932–1933 the Surveyor General's office (*maanmittaushallitus*) counted 61,964 lakes using maps made on a 1:400,000 scale. This meant that only bodies of water at least 220 yards (200 meters) in diameter showed up on the map and were counted. After World War II, when Finland lost Viipuri Province to the Soviet Union, the 6,721 lakes in Viipuri were subtracted, leaving 55,243.

Many suspected that this count was too low, especially since Sweden was estimating her own lakes at 100,000 and Norway at 200,000. In 1982 a professor of ecology and environment at Jyväskylä University in Central Finland organized a seminar on the history of Finnish lakes. It was decided to make a new count, using 3,712 larger and more detailed area maps. In June 1985 the new count was certified: 187,888.

Even that count does not include every body of water in Finland. Ponds or lakes smaller than 600 sq. yd. (500 sq. m.) were excluded. The average size of Finland's many lakes is 44.5 acres (18 hectares). In contrast, the size of Norway's average lake is 14.8 acres (6 hectares).

only a short distance to St. Petersburg (now Leningrad). Not only matches but butter, furs, bobbins, and plywood followed this trade route. Logs often stopped at Kotka on the coast—192 mi. (320 km.) south of Kuopio—for processing and export.

While trucks and airplanes now transport a lot of goods, the inland waterways are still in use. During the summer the lakes become shipping lanes for boats and floating lanes for the lumber industry, which sends logs to sawmills and papermills.

Though the floating of logs is seasonal, the lumber industry is an important year-round enterprise. During the winter the trees are felled, the branches removed, and the logs cut into lengths of about eight feet. Each farm or company has its own seal, which is cut into the end of the log. Then the log is dragged—in the past by horses and now by tractors or trucks—to the nearest waterway, where it is piled on the thick ice. In the late spring, when the lakes melt, the logs begin their float, sometimes singly if down a narrow river, sometimes tied together in bundles, that may float free or be pulled by tugboats. The waterways used for floating lumber are so long, they would stretch around the equator if they were put together.

The Lumberjack

The work of the lumberjack—whether felling trees in winter or guiding the logs in the spring and summer—is strenuous, and the Finns admire it. It combines a spirit of adventurousness with hard labor in close communion with nature. Logs may become jammed at bends in streams, and the lumberjacks use long poles to free them, jumping from log to log to reach the trouble spot. They wear spiked boots to keep from slipping, but the work is very dangerous, especially when there is a torrent of rushing water. In the past many farmers worked in lumber

Since the surface of Lake Saimaa is 250 ft. (76 m.) above sea level, the Saimaa Canal has eight locks, three on the Finnish side and five on the Soviet side. Finnish Ministry for Foreign Affairs/Press and Cultural Center

camps during the winter months to earn extra income, while the women ran the farms. Today the timber industry has become mechanized, but lumberjacking is still an occupation requiring special training and strength.

Forest Industry

As far back as the Middle Ages the Finns were exporting round logs and hewn goods across the Baltic Sea. The first water-driven sawmill is mentioned as early as 1545, and by the eighteenth century there was a logging industry. Today there is concern about forestry planning, and Finns are increasingly aware of the impact of industrial pollution from Germany and from Finland itself.

Just a generation ago the forest industry accounted for 75 percent of Finnish exports. Today the proportion is about 35 percent, reflecting the diversification of the Finnish economy. Still Finland accounts for 15 percent of all the paper and cardboard produced in the world, including some newsprint used in the United States. *The New York Times*, the *Philadelphia Inquirer*, and the *Miami Herald* are printed in part on Finnish paper.

Cabin in the Woods

The beauty of the Lake District has inspired many artists. The water route between Tampere and Lahti is called The Poet's Way. Johan Ludvig Runeberg (1804–1877), the national poet, often hiked in the

This farm amid the forests in eastern Savo is typical of the pioneer patterns of clearing a homestead near a lake. Farmers traditionally harvested some of their forests each winter to supplement their incomes. Finnish Tourist Board

Punkaharju area and had a home in the unspoiled woods of Saarijärvi, north of Jyväskylä. Many artists chose to live at least part of the year in the wilderness of the Lake District, including the sculptor Emil Wikstrøm (1864–1942) and Akseli Gallen-Kallela (1865–1931), a painter and architect who designed two houses for himself: one near Helsinki and the other in Ruovesi in the middle of the Lake District. Kalela, as the house is called, is a huge log building, considered the most remarkable example of romantic wood architecture in Finland. It was here that Gallen-Kallela produced the first examples of Finnish graphic art and painted themes from Finnish folklore. The famous composer Jean Sibelius (1865–1957) and others liked to visit their "hermit" friend in his beautiful setting in the woods.

Even today many Finns spend part of the year in country places. These second homes may be just one-room cottages or ordinary houses with several rooms, including bedrooms upstairs. Many of them are

Saimaa Canal

It took several thousand laborers over ten summers and funds equivalent to one year's national budget to build the 35-mile (56-kilometer) Saimaa Canal linking Finland with Russia. Czar Alexander II opened the waterway in 1856, amidst statues of the Roman God Neptune and Väinämöinen, the principal hero of Finland's national epic, the *Kalevala*.

The canal was closed in 1944 when it was bisected by the new Finnish-Soviet border. After negotiations and much reconstruction, the canal was reopened in 1968 for both commerce and pleasure.

quite rustic, without running water or electricity. Water is fetched from a lake or a well, and food is cooked on a wood-burning or camp stove. It is rare for a Finnish cottage not to have a sauna, the Finnish bath-house. Most cottages are isolated to be secluded and peaceful. The Finns like the simplicity and do not mind the lack of amenities.

At their country houses the Finns like to go berrying and mushroom picking. In earlier times these foods were a means of survival, especially in eastern Finland. During World War II the mushrooms known as "milk caps" provided an important source of nutrients for many. Today they may be picked for mushroom sausages or for salads and stews, and berries add special color to festive occasions.

Culture Areas

The Lake District includes three "culture areas," Häme, Savo, and Karelia, in which different dialects, foods, customs, and regional stereo-types developed and persist to this day. Häme people are often de-scribed as slow, cautious farmers noted for their highly decorated homes. Savo people are considered quick to laugh, have a rich dialect full of elaborate descriptions, and live in small, plain homes. Karelians are known for their friendliness, family loyalty, and rich folktales and songs. Hämeenlinna, literally the "castle of Häme," is considered the cultural center of Häme. Savonlinna, the "castle of Savo," and Kuopio are centers of Savo. Since World War II Joensuu and Imatra have become the centers of Karelia, replacing Viipuri, now in the Soviet Union. There is still a flavor of old Karelia in the marketplace in Joensuu, where men in high riding boots tell lively stories of the past.

CULTURE AREAS OF THE LAKE DISTRICT

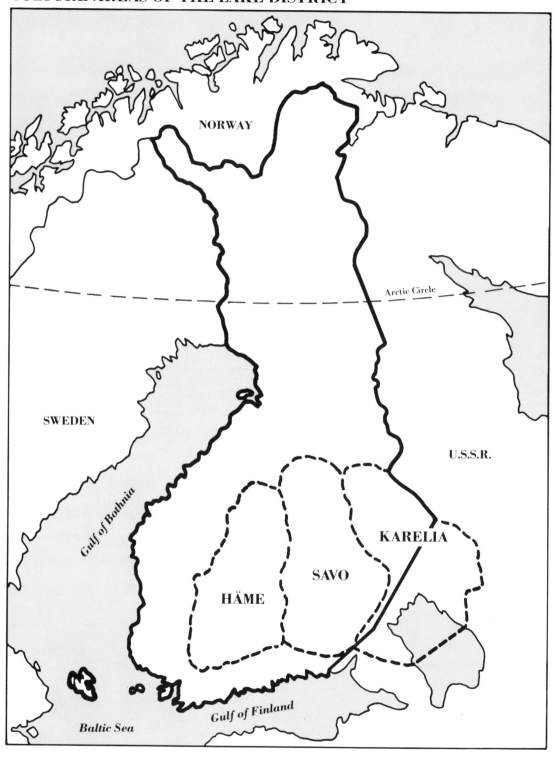

The Coastal Lowlands

The coastal lowlands in the south and west of Finland are the richest part of the country. Here there were the first farms, the first towns, the first castles, the first centers of international exchange.

The lowlands lie along the two arms of the Baltic Sea: the Gulf of Bothnia along the western shores between Finland and Sweden, and the Gulf of Finland in the south between Finland and Estonia. The rugged and irregular coastline, which is approximately 682 mi. (1,100 km.) long, is continually changing as the land reemerges. The granite bedrock, so characteristic of the whole country, reveals itself in its most dramatic form here in the great rocks of the coast and outlying islands.

The Golden Horseshoe

The southwest corner of the coastal plains is called "the golden horseshoe of Finland." It has the best climate, the most luxuriant vegetation, and the widest range of fauna. Its abundance of well-kept fields and fat cattle make it the country's finest agricultural region.

The coastal plains contain lakes and forests, as throughout Finland, but they are fewer than elsewhere. Small hills and valleys are characteristic of the south. On the western coast, in contrast, the plains of Ostrobothnia are mostly flat and consist of clay that has recently been reclaimed from the sea. These cultivated clay lands are split by many rivers, including the Kokemäenjoki and Aura, which overflow in the spring and autumn. Some years the Ostrobothnian farmers have to harvest their crops by boat before the floods recede. Still, the harvests are more bountiful than from the stony soil of the rest of Finland.

The Corner of the Estates

Along the river valleys there are remains of Iron Age settlements. These were eventually replaced by the castles and churches of the Middle Ages, then the farmsteads and rustic villages of a century or so ago.

The countryside has been cultivated for more than a thousand years. In the sixteenth and seventeenth centuries the King of Sweden-Finland gave nobles large tracts of land in this region, and Swedish-speaking Finns still call this section "the corner of the estates." Most of the estates have lost their large acreage, but many of the manor houses remain and some are still owned by descendants of the original nobles. Today Finland's principal orchards grow fruit where nobles once hunted.

In the west in Ostrobothnia, Swedish farming settlements grew up side by side with Finnish settlements, creating a unified Western Finnish culture despite two separate languages. Several Ostrobothnian municipalities have a majority of Swedish speakers.

Sailing Traditions

The people of the coast have had more contact with the rest of Europe than other Finns. Expeditions of Vikings, or *Varyags*, passed through the Finnish archipelago heading east to Lake Ladoga and then south as far as Byzantium. Historians suspect that some inhabitants of the area now called Finland joined these expeditions in the tenth and eleventh centuries. Finns have had a special place in the mythology of seafarers ever since. It was said that a sailing vessel should have at least one Finn, usually a sailmaker, for it was believed that he could calm storms or call up the wind at will.

As early as the Middle Ages the Finns were sailing their own ships in the Baltic Sea. The first record of a Finnish ship entering an English port dates from the time of Queen Elizabeth I. By the seventeenth century Finland was a major shipbuilding country with dry docks along the coast, making ships to sell to Sweden and foreign countries. After 1765, when the towns on the western coast were given permission to export tar directly to foreign countries, Finland's seaborne traffic experienced an unprecedented rise. Soon a new forest product—timber—joined the export traffic.

Today Finland produces luxury liners, sailboats, and yachts that have navigated the world many times over. Since the 1930's Finland has been especially known for its icebreakers, examples of the technological expertise of Finnish industry in designing equipment adapted for operation under difficult conditions. One shipyard recently completed a research vessel for exploration in Antarctica; another specializes in the construction of offshore oil rigs.

Turku, Finland's First Administrative Center

Finland was first administered from Turku, located at the mouth of the River Aura near the coastline in the southwest. Compared with Central Europe, urban life is relatively recent in Finland. Even in Turku (Swedish: Åbo), Finland's oldest city, urbanization did not begin until sometime during the fourteenth century. Once it began, however, Turku took

Anchored at the River Aura in Turku, Finland's third-largest city, is the old sailing ship the Suomen Joutsen (Swan of Finland). *The white-hulled vessel, which was once a naval cadet ship, now serves as a school of navigation.*   Finnish Tourist Board

on all the characteristics of a thriving cosmopolitan center. With the establishment of a bishop's seat and cathedral, the influence of the Church grew and the artisan class expanded. Turku was a rest stop on the "royal road" that linked Stockholm and St. Petersburg, and even today it remains Finland's chief passenger-ship terminal. Finland's first university was founded in Turku in 1640. It was also a mill-processing center for the neighboring inland farms, as were other port towns, and an old windmill still stands in the center of the city to remind modern dwellers of the past.

Tar: An Important Early Export

Vaasa, a major port on the Gulf of Bothnia, was very busy for several centuries supplying tar to shipbuilders in Great Britain, France, and the Netherlands. Tar was Finland's first major export, and for a couple of centuries most of the ships of the British navy were coated with Finnish tar. Much of the tar came from the interior down the difficult eighty-mile course of the Oulujoki (Oulu River). Many tarboat captains became local heroes from their tales about navigating the river. Today, fur farms and greenhouse cultivation have replaced tar burning as means of livelihood for those who do not own farms, but the port cities continue to stress their tar history for tourists and history buffs alike.

Many towns along the Gulf of Finland have become export harbors. Kotka, a new city where the Kymi River enters the Gulf, is now the largest harbor in Finland and is noted for its tall storage silos. The famous Finnish architect Alvar Aalto (1898–1976) designed the Sunila sulphate mill near Kotka, from the storage yards and ponds through which wood enters the plant area to the dock for delivery to ocean-going freighters, along with supporting housing for employees and executives.

Tar, which was used to seal the bottoms of wooden ships, was made by slowly burning pine trees in large covered pits. As the wood decomposed, gases were created, which then condensed into tar. National Board of Antiquities of Finland

Between Kotka and Helsinki lies Porvoo, one of Finland's oldest coastal towns. It was an important trading post years before its official founding in 1346 on a strategic site at the mouth of the Porvoo River. In a fifteenth-century cathedral, a massive stone structure with walls six feet thick, Czar Alexander I opened the Diet (Parliament) in 1809 and declared that Finland would be an autonomous grand duchy of Russia, and he would be the Grand Duke.

Helsinki: Daughter of the Baltic

Finland's capital, Helsinki, is a great coastal city. It is surrounded on three sides by sea and islands, and bays extend deep into the town. The city covers an area of 141 sq. mi. (365 sq. km.), half of which is water. Steamers from Sweden and Germany arrive in the very center of the city and moor in the south harbor close to the marketplace. The ships that berth along the waterfront are one reason why Helsinki calls herself "the daughter of the Baltic."

When it became the capital of Finland in 1812, Helsinki was just a small village with a population of about 4,000. Today there are close to 500,000 residents. Most of Finland's town dwellers have always lived in the port cities of the south and southwest coasts, although they also lived in centers, such as Tampere, in the interior.

In the last half of the twentieth century a great movement of people to the cities has occurred. The proportion of town dwellers to rural dwellers has changed dramatically. In 1950 only 33 percent of the Finnish population lived in cities; now 62 percent do. Remote districts in the north and east where farms were scattered were affected first, then larger villages. Some people migrated to regional capitals, but the major pull was to Helsinki. One million of Finland's 4.9 million people now live in the Greater Helsinki Area.

Helsinki is Finland's largest and most cosmopolitan city, and as a governmental, diplomatic, and cultural center it continues the innovative role the coastal areas have played throughout Finnish history and prehistory.

Today Helsinki is known as an international meeting place where nations from the East and the West can find common ground. Two buildings, visual reminders of Finland's history as part of both the East and West, dominate Helsinki's skyline. The Lutheran Cathedral, a sign

The moment the sun appears, Finns prefer to be out of doors. A favorite pastime is having coffee at one of the many outdoor cafés, such as this one in Esplanade Park near the harbor in Helsinki.   Finnish Tourist Board

that for six hundred years Finland was a part of the Kingdom of Sweden, is a dazzling white structure that stands atop Senate Square. Nearby, overlooking the south harbor, perched on a steep hill, is the enormous red-brick Uspensky Cathedral, built by the Czars for the Eastern Orthodox community. It now serves as the cathedral of the Finnish Orthodox Church. Between the two lies the open-air market square where fishermen and farmers trade their wares with the city dwellers.

On the dock at Helsinki's south harbor one can buy the makings of a typical Finnish meal—new potatoes and freshly caught Baltic fish. Finnish Tourist Board

The Coastal Archipelago

The mass of islands along Finland's coast constitutes an amazing jigsaw puzzle that reveals Finland's geological evolution and social and military history. In the outer archipelago a new island may surface in the course of a person's lifetime, or a small crack in a rock may grow to be four feet wide.

Thousands of Granite Shapes

In the southwest the broken coastline gradually yields to the Finnish archipelago, which is one of the largest and most spectacular in the world. It contains tens of thousands of granite islands. Some are only large rocks. Others are skerries (small rocky islets) with small trees and shrubs, which are landing places for seabirds. Yet others are small islands with perhaps one to a dozen summer cottages or fishing huts.

Finally there are large islands such as the Ålands, with the capital at Mariehamn (in Finnish: Maarianhamina).

Finland contains more islands than any other country in the world. In a recent count, the total number of islands in Finland came to almost as many as the lakes: 179,584! Forty-five percent are in the Baltic Sea, making the archipelago one of the densest in the world. The islands are so plentiful and varied that the Finnish language has at least forty-four different words for them. There is a specific word, for example, for an especially wooded island or an especially small island or an island that is uninhabited.

Everywhere along the Finnish coast islands poke through the water, demanding careful sailing.   Finnish Tourist Board

An Obstacle Course   During all seasons—even in the severest winter, with the help of icebreakers—large ocean liners make daily trips from Finland through the archipelago to Stockholm or northern Germany. To navigate through the intricate maze of islands requires skill and good maps. Not surprisingly, the art of mapmaking was perfected in this region of Finland. By the middle of the eighteenth century the militia had a topographical corps, which first surveyed the archipelago and then the rest of the countryside. They noted everything—from the navigability of waterways to the fordability of streams to the details of secret woodland paths. With or without maps, Finns were said to have developed an almost magical cunning to be able to maneuver through their many obstacle courses.

The early interest in maps was sparked by military concerns. As Napoleon said, the Ålands were the key to the Baltic. By the end of the nineteenth century Finland was the first European country to have produced a detailed national atlas with maps on climate, agriculture, fishing, dialects, and migrations.

The Åland Islands

The name Åland comes from an old Scandinavian word, *ahvaland*, meaning water-land (*ahvenanmaa* in Finnish). The Ålands have a warmer climate than the rest of Finland because of their southern location and have a varied plant life, including oak woods and hazel groves that give shelter to anemone, primrose, viola, bluebell, and lily-of-the-valley. On the rockier seashores facing the winds are wild rose, wild red currant, and raspberry.

Vegetables such as onions, Chinese cabbage, potatoes, and sugar beets are grown on Åland for sale on the Finnish mainland. Though there is not much land for gardening, the soil is productive, and the somewhat longer growing season makes farming less risky than in many places on the mainland.

Throughout history, the Ålands have been a base for sailors and fishermen. Clipper ships from Turku and Åland have sailed world-wide. Most of Finland's fishing fleets are docked in Åland or at the Turku harbor. Seventy percent of Finland's fishing catch comes from the Baltic Sea, and of the approximately 32 pounds of fish a Finn eats annually, half consists of Baltic herring.

Prehistory   Archaeologists believe that the first immigrants to the Åland Islands came from the region of Turku, 60 mi. (100 km.) away, since the same kinds of tools and pottery have been found in the Stone Age sites. Nobody knows whether the boats on which they came were hollowed-out tree trunks, boats made of skins, or rafts. The early population could not have been very large, since only the peaks of what are now the north Åland mountains were then sticking out of the sea. The first inhabitants survived on seals, fish, and birds. Wooden fish-hooks were used for fishing, bows and arrows for hunting birds, and spears with bone harpoon tips for hunting seals.

By the Viking Era (around A.D. 1,000), the Åland Islands were one of the most densely populated areas in Scandinavia, since they were directly in the middle of the trade route between Sweden and Russia.

Fortifications   Even though the treacherous channels of the archipelago provided some protection from foreign invaders, the islands also bristle with man-made stone fortresses. Major fortifications were built in the Åland Islands and outside Helsinki, but there were smaller forts throughout the archipelago. One of Finland's most formidable medieval forts, Kastelholm in the Åland Islands, may have been built as early as the second half of the twelfth century; it is made from natural local stone, with massive walls and a lookout tower, on the rise of a small island. It is possible that this first fort was built by Crusaders, possibly from Denmark, who used it as a stopping-off place for their rowing ships on the way to Finland. In later years it was expanded to include a castle and many houses.

Kastelholm was once visited by the Swedish kings Gustavus Vasa, Gustavus Adolphus II, and the luckless Eric XIV, who spent some time in the dungeon. Partially destroyed by fire in the eighteenth century, one wing has been rebuilt for the Åland Historical Museum. Finnish Tourist Board

The Gibraltar of the North

In the eighteenth century Sweden decided to erect a great sea fortress near Helsinki to block Russia's westward expansion. Suomenlinna ("Finland's castle") was built on five connecting islands, and the fortress was called the Gibraltar of the North.

In 1809, when the Russians advanced from Helsinki, the fortress surrendered without a shot. Perhaps the officers believed the faked reports that Russian reinforcements had arrived on the mainland and that everyone else had surrendered. Suomenlinna still houses military barracks, a naval base, and naval repair yard, as well as museums and a theater.

The Ålanders have always felt close to Sweden, and when Finland declared her independence in 1917, many Ålanders wanted to be united with Sweden. Residents petitioned the King and government of Sweden, but Finland protested. The issue was submitted to the League of Nations, which decided in 1921 that Finland should be granted sovereignty and that the Ålands should be given important guarantees.

An Autonomous Province   Åland has had an autonomy act since 1952. It guarantees the preservation of the province's language (Swedish) and self-government on internal matters. The province has its own flag, which, since 1970, has been flown alongside the flags of the Nordic countries at regional events. In 1984 Åland acquired the right to produce its own postage stamps.

The province is a neutral demilitarized zone whose inhabitants are exempt from military service. The Ålands are sometimes referred to as the Peace Islands.

Close to Sweden

Some parts of the western archipelago are closer to Sweden than to
Finland. Ålanders are Swedish speakers, and the cultural ties with
Sweden have always been strong. From the middle of the
seventeenth century to the end of the nineteenth century, Eckerö,
the westernmost district of Åland, provided mail service by rowboat
over the Åland Sea to Grisslehamn in Sweden, 25 mi. (40 km.)
away. Two hundred lives were lost in storms during the 250 years
this postal service operated. The mail service is commemorated by
an annual rowing and sailing competition, the Mail Boat Regatta,
every June.

Social Change in the Outer Archipelago

In earlier times the ideal of the people in the outer archipelago was to
be completely self-sufficient. They fished, grew vegetables, and kept
cows for milk. They had enough to feed themselves but did not have
extra produce for sale. In the 1880's, when manufactured cloth, paraffin
lamps, coffee, sugar, and agricultural equipment became available, it
became harder to live without surplus crops to sell.

By the mid-1920's, motorboats came on the market. They became
important for fishing—and for smuggling bootlegged liquor during the
years when the national government outlawed the sale of hard liquor
(1919–1932). In 1958 trawling boats were introduced. Some farmers
began to grow crops for sale: first onions and cucumbers, later tomatoes.

But the hard truth is that with each new development, the difficulty of living in the outer archipelago increased. When electricity went out or delivery boats did not arrive, the islanders felt all the more isolated.

As they saw that their costs were increasing while their standard of living was still not keeping up with that of the mainland, many islanders

Though the Åland Islands are the most southern part of Finland they are sometimes colder than the mainland because of the winds off the Baltic Sea. Hannu Vanhanen

Fishing has always been an important activity on the Ålands. Today commercial fleets and sportfishers have mostly replaced the small boat team. The time from the fifteenth of April to the fifteenth of June is reserved for nesting sea birds, and fishing from land is forbidden then.   Finnish Tourist Board

migrated to the center of Åland or to Sweden or to the Swedish-speaking parts of Finland. This push from the edges of the archipelago toward the center is a trend in the Ålands and throughout Finland. But some few hardy souls still live in the outer archipelago and wave as the boats go by.

Between
East and West:
The Birth of
a Nation

Finland's history is a history of struggle to overcome the odds of its harsh physical environment and political situation. Using simple tools and much hard labor, settlers cleared lands in the wilderness inhabited by wolves and bears. Once they were settled, they were often called on to fight: first against invaders, and then, for many years, for the Swedish crown. Independence was accompanied by a bitter civil war, and twenty years after the Republic was established, Finland was at war with the Soviet Union in defense of Finnish lands. These struggles have resulted in a nation with a strong sense of its own identity and a commitment to democracy. Finland has learned to survive between East and West. It has learned the importance of a stable neutrality, with good neighbor and trade relations with both the Eastern and Western nations.

Finland has always been a northern outpost between East and West. Its culture and society have been shaped by migrations of people and ideas from the east, west, and south. Because of its location on the shores of the Baltic Sea, a major sea route in northern Europe, Finland has been important to Sweden and to Russia, who each wanted control of the waterway, and later to Germany and to the Soviet Union. For centuries foreign powers fought on and for control of Finland's territory. The Finnish people have sought, often with great hardship and loss of lives, to develop and maintain their own identity and nationhood: not to be Swedes or Russians, but to be Finns.

Early Inhabitants

Just as America was inhabited by American Indians who crossed the Bering Straits long before the arrival of Columbus, so too Finland was settled through a series of migrations long before it became part of European history. The sparse settlements clustered around rivers, away from the coasts, and dotted the countryside from the Gulf of Bothnia to Lake Ladoga.

The early inhabitants of Finland lived in relative isolation. Their major contact with the outside world was with traders who took animal pelts to the markets of Rome, Byzantium, and the Frankish kingdom and brought back salt, iron, and weapons.

At the time the Vikings were passing by Finland's shores (approximately A.D. 800–1100), the tribal peoples lived in self-sufficient communities, were accustomed to making their own decisions, forged their own plows and swords in their own smithies, and trusted their own gods. They worshiped their supreme god of lightning, Ukko, and other gods, such as Ahti, the god who gave fish, and Ilmarinen, who ruled the weather. They had shrines where they sacrificed grain, fish, and live animals to the gods.

The early tribes (known as the Finns Proper, the Häme, and the

Karelians) were subdivided into clans with lands held in common. When one of its members was attacked, the clan took swift revenge. The tribal leaders received special burials but did not have the status or authority of kings.

The Coming of Christianity

Though sparsely populated, Finland's location and natural resources were important enough for it to become a battleground between rival religions and foreign powers. The Germans, Danes, Swedes, and Russians all made expeditions along the Finnish coast to try to gain control over trade in the period between A.D. 900 and 1200. These invaders recognized that the Baltic Sea, which connects with the Volkhov–Dnieper waterway in Russia, provided a major water route into and out of Russia and a link even to the faraway Byzantine Empire at Constantinople. For the Russians in particular, the Baltic Sea was crucial, since it was Russia's only outlet to northern Europe. Control of the Baltic has been an important goal to the Russians ever since.

The rivalry between the Eastern Orthodox Church in Constantinople and the Western Catholic Church in Rome, dating back to the division of the Roman Empire into Eastern and Western halves, encouraged warfare among Finnish peoples and between Swedes and Russians.

The Pope in Rome was anxious to establish a foothold in Finland before the Finns embraced the doctrines of the Eastern Orthodox Church, and he urged the Swedish bishops to convert their eastern neighbors. Around 1157 the Swedes launched the first Finnish "Crusade," led by Bishop Henry of Uppsala. The crusade was not immediately successful. Bishop Henry was slain with an ax by a prosperous peasant named Lalli during the first winter—on January 20 on a frozen lake, according to tradition. But an association that was to bind Fin-

Quarta materia de nauigatione regis et episcopi in finlandiam

A woodcut showing the English-born Bishop Henry of Uppsala and King Eric of Sweden crossing the Baltic Sea on their way to convert the Finns. National Board of Antiquities of Finland

land's destiny with Sweden for over six hundred years had begun.

After Henry's murder, a few priests were left behind in the southwest corner of Finland. At the same time, Eastern Orthodox missionaries and traders sent by the Russian Prince of Novgorod were gaining converts in eastern Finland. The oldest Finnish words dealing with Christianity, *risti* (cross) and *pakana* (pagan), are of Russian origin.

The Swedish missionaries slowly made headway in erecting churches in the place of pagan sacrificial groves, and they organized military expeditions to the east. Early attempts to advance past the River Neva were stopped by Prince Alexander of Novgorod. But the Swedes were successful in colonizing the western and southern coasts of Finland during the thirteenth century.

The Conquest of West Karelia

Sweden continued to eye lands farther east. In 1293 Swedish expeditionary forces reached as far as Viipuri, where they built a castle on the site of an old trading post. From this base at Viipuri the Swedes sought to conquer all of Karelia. In 1300 they got close to the present city of Leningrad, where they built another fortress, but they had to surrender a couple of years later under enemy harassment and the ravages of disease. This territory contested by Sweden and Novgorod (later Russia) was to see many other battles between 1300 and 1945.

The Russians counterattacked in 1311 and marched all the way to Häme, getting as far as Turku a few years later. All this fighting and counterfighting was disruptive to trade in the Baltic, and German merchants, acting as mediators, eventually arranged a peace. In 1323 the first written agreement between Sweden and Russia was drawn up. The Pähkinäsaari Treaty of 1323 divided Karelia between Sweden and Novgorod.

Part of the Kingdom of Sweden

With the signing of the treaty, Finland became an integral part of the Kingdom of Sweden and of Western Christianity. To the east of the new frontier, however, there still lived a large Finnish population who belonged to the Eastern Orthodox faith. Finland shared Sweden's laws, religion, and system of taxation. As early as 1362 representatives of the Finnish people were granted the right to vote in elections of the Swedish

King, and Finland was represented in Parliament, just like the other provinces. Through Sweden, Finland became part of the European community, with increased trade and university education abroad.

In comparison to rural people in most of Europe, the Finnish *talonpoika* (peasant) was relatively free. Finnish peasants were never serfs. On the other hand, Finland suffered more harshly than Sweden proper when Swedish power was challenged, and Finns were recruited onto the battlefield time and time again to defend Swedish interests.

Viipuri Castle, established in 1293, was at the easternmost corner of the kingdom. Severin Folkman's 1885 painting shows Prince Karl Knutson leaving to go to Stockholm for the election in 1448 in which he became King of the Swedes. National Board of Antiquities of Finland

The Birth of the Centralized State

At first Finland was simply Sweden's Østerland, the land in the east. In the sixteenth century King Gustavus Vasa took a more personal interest and made a tour of inspection. At the end of his visit in 1556, he made Finland a duchy and set up Prince Johan, his second son, as head of the court in Turku castle. Prince Johan set out to learn Finnish and established a brilliant court life in Turku, such as Finland had never seen before.

During Gustavus Vasa's reign (1523–1560), Lutheranism came to Finland. Vasa embraced the Protestant Reformation, made himself head of the Church of Sweden, and replaced Latin with the local language in church services, a very important development for the Finnish speakers in Finland.

The Church in Finland

The Christian Church has played a crucial role in shaping Finnish history and national identity. The missionaries took away most of the Finns' early beliefs and rituals (though they persisted longer than the priests wanted to admit), but the Church also looked after the social welfare of its followers. Granite churches were built; wood-carvers modeled saints; and church leaders took books to Finland. Through the canonization of Bishop Henry, Finland acquired its own saint, which made Turku a place of pilgrimage. In one hymn the birthplace of Jesus was changed from a stable to a sauna. Later the parish was used as the basis for local government and administration.

Under the influence of the Lutheran Reformation, the first books in the Finnish language were produced. Michael Agricola (1510–1557), a young Finn who had been to Germany and studied under Martin Luther,

was instrumental in furthering the new religious teachings. As Bishop of Turku he insisted there be a prayer book in the people's own language. The prayer book carried this motto: "He who sees into all hearts, He assuredly also understands a Finnish prayer."

Agricola also translated the New Testament into Finnish in 1548 and thus gave Finland its first literary language. Just as significant was his publication of an ABC book to teach the uneducated to read. Altogether ten books in Finnish were published during his years at Turku.

Finland in Early Modern Times

During the sixteenth, seventeenth, and eighteenth centuries, the Finns paid a heavy price to further Sweden's ambition to be a great world power. They were called upon to fight in innumerable wars; and while some of the campaigns were fought outside Finland's borders, many were fought against Russia, which meant that Finland was the first arena of battle. Especially destructive among the recurring conflicts with the Russians were the wars of 1554–1557, the Twenty-Five Years' War (1570–1595), the war of 1609–1617, another war from 1656 to 1658, and the long and tragic Northern War, 1700–1721. There was fighting against Russia again from 1741 to 1743 and from 1788 to 1790.

The Finns fought bravely. They had a reputation as fierce soldiers with strong horses and fearless leaders. But their sacrifices earned them little. Rewards usually went to Swedish generals, who received vast grants of Finnish territory to establish estates.

The wooden bell towers of churches were also used for people to leave guns in before entering the church in pioneer days. Since 1923 freedom of religion has been guaranteed by law. Ninety percent of Finns belong to the Evangelical Lutheran Church. Parishes levy on their members ecclesiastical taxes, which are collected by the civil authorities. Hannu Vanhanen

By 1654 approximately three fifths of Finland was in possession of Finland-Swedish nobles, who grew in wealth and power. Finnish ceased to be spoken at all in cultivated homes, and Swedish became the required language in the law courts and in the schools. Many families changed their names to Latin or Swedish names.

NEW SWEDEN   In the seventeenth century, Finns took part in the short-lived Swedish colony in the New World on the banks of the Delaware River, organized by the New Sweden Company between 1638 and 1656, which was later peacefully absorbed by the British. Some Finns stayed on in the colonies, and among their descendants was John Morton of Pennsylvania, who signed the Declaration of Independence.

The constant warfare brought injury and disaster, as well as a heavy burden of taxation. Farmers who could not pay these taxes had to give up their lands and become crofters. (A crofter, *torppari* in Finnish, was a tenant who paid his rent to the landowner in the form of a certain number of days' work. Usually a croft could provide the tenant with a living. A smaller plot of leased land, intended to provide residence only, was called a cottage and its inhabitants cottagers.)

Devastating food shortages were frequent. A particularly severe famine occurred at the end of the seventeenth century. The winter of 1694 turned extraordinarily cold, and when the crops failed the next year, there were massive numbers of deaths. In the years 1695 to 1697, about one third of the population died of starvation. In one parish near Turku the church bell cracked during this famine because of its ceaseless tolling for the dead.

The Founding of St. Petersburg and the Collapse of Sweden

With the reign of Peter the Great of Russia (1689–1725), a new era in Finnish history began. In 1699 Peter concluded a secret alliance with Poland and Denmark against Sweden and, after conquering Swedish Livonia and Ingria, ordered the founding of St. Petersburg (now Leningrad) at the mouth of the River Neva on lands that had originally been occupied by Finns. Peter's decision to build his city on the coast of the Baltic Sea showed his determination to expand westward. For two hundred years, from 1714 to 1917, the seat of the Russian government was in St. Petersburg, not in Moscow.

Peter's armies invaded Finland during the Great War of the North (1700–1721). For the last five years of the war, all of Finland was under Russian occupation. Finns were taken to Russia in captivity. Few ever returned, and Russia won Viipuri, Finland's most important market town and seaport, in the Treaty of Uusikaupunki in 1721. The writer Topelius (1818–1898) vividly described the ravages of the countryside:

When refugees returned to their homes they found the roads destroyed, the bridges broken, no horses, no food, the whole country a desert. The houses were either burned down or roofless and windowless, their contents sacked. The wells were filled with earth, the plough lands were overgrown with forest, birds had their nests in abandoned churches.

The destruction and lawlessness of the Russian occupation was so harsh that this period has been called The Great Wrath.

At the same time, Sweden was weakened by dynastic struggles. It was quickly losing its position as a great power. In 1741 the whole of Finland was occupied once more by Russia, and more lands were lost in a treaty of 1743. When Sweden and Russia fought over Finland again from 1788 to 1790, many Finns started to doubt that Sweden could protect the country.

Some Finns plotted to create an independent Finland under Russian protection, but they did not win wide support. Still, the idea that Finland had an identity of its own apart from Sweden was beginning to develop. Henrik Gabriel Porthan (1739–1804), a professor at the University of Turku, encouraged his students to study the past and the potential of their homeland. He was the first scholar of Finnish history, language, and folklore.

Porthan foresaw the dangers that lay ahead. Writing to the poet F. M. Franzen, he said:

We must pray to God that Russia will succeed in situating its capital in Constantinople. Then it might leave remote Finland in peace under the scepter of Sweden. But, now that its capital city is located so near, I am afraid that Finland will sooner or later fall under the power of Russia. I hope that I won't have to witness this misfortune, but you may live to see it, you who are young.

Porthan died in 1804. In 1807 Alexander I of Russia and Napoleon I of France agreed that Europe should be divided between their two great realms, the same pact made over a hundred years later by Stalin and Hitler.

In 1808 Russia invaded Finland. While many soldiers and lower-ranking commanders fought hard, Sweden was preoccupied with safeguarding its interests in Norway, and much of the war consisted of a series of retreats. The Czar encouraged the Finns to give up the fight and to consent to a proposal for an autonomous Finland within the Russian Empire. In February 1809 Czar Alexander I issued a proclamation convening a special session of the Diet (Parliament) at Porvoo. Alexander I promised to uphold the Evangelical-Lutheran faith and the constitutional law and rights of Finland. The Finns for their part swore an oath of allegiance to the new ruler. The 600-year union between Finland and Sweden was broken. A peace treaty was signed between Sweden and Russia on September 17, 1809, but it simply acknowledged what had already happened. From then on Finland would be part of Russia until the Finnish Parliament declared its independence on December 6, 1917.

At the opening ceremony of the Diet of 1809 at the cathedral in Porvoo, Czar Alexander I addressed the Finnish representatives. On the awning above the throne is the double-headed eagle of Russia. (Painting by E. Theining) National Board of Antiquities of Finland

BORDERS OF FINLAND FROM 1323 TO 1944

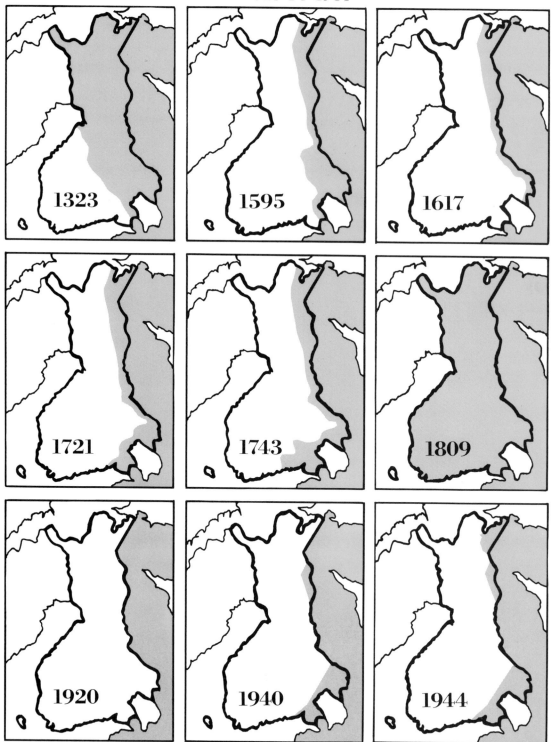

Shaded areas governed by Russia/U.S.S.R.

A Grand Duchy of the Russian Empire

When Finland was annexed by Russia, the disaster Porthan had feared did not come. Especially during the early years, Finland was freer to manage its domestic affairs than it had been under Swedish rule. Finns were exempt from military service and had the protection of the Imperial Russian Army. No longer did they have to fight Sweden's battles with few if any rewards. Except for a brief bombardment of some of Finland's forts by the British fleet during the Crimean War (1854–1855), the Finnish people experienced ninety years of peace, something they had never had.

Finland kept its old constitution, its two languages (Swedish and Finnish), its religion, and its legal system (The Law of the Swedish Realm). Even the Bank of Finland was separate from Russian banks, and after 1860 Finland had its own currency. The Czar was persuaded to restore to Finland the territory lost in 1721, including Viipuri Province (called Old Finland). Though Alexander I ruled an empire whose common people were still in a condition of serfdom, the Finnish peasants were left free.

Russia demanded political loyalty from the Finns and, with minor exceptions, received it. Industry developed to supply the duty-free Russian market and, especially with the opening of the Saimaa Canal in 1856, linking Finland's inland waterways with the Gulf of Finland, the eastern Finnish rural economy prospered. Tar, timber, and finally paper were sold abroad. Soon ships and steam engines were being manufactured.

The first sewing machines were imported into Finland about 1865, and the need for bobbins soon expanded into a major processing industry. By 1900 Kuopio was the bobbin-making capital of Europe. National Board of Antiquities of Finland

The Czar was represented in Finland by a Governor General. An Administrative Council and a Senate composed of Finnish subjects appointed by the Czar directed the duchy's internal affairs. The man selected for the first governor-generalship was not a Russian but a Finland Swede, Colonel Sprengtporten (1740–1819), who had earlier fled to Russia with the idea of establishing a Finnish republic under Russian leadership. After Sprengtporten, the Governors General were all Russians.

A New Capital: Helsinki

Under Swedish rule Finland's capital had been Stockholm. Turku, on the Baltic coast, had been the province's center, with a bishop's seat, a university, and a court of appeals. The Czar called for the creation of a new capital on the Gulf of Finland, nearer to St. Petersburg. He ordered Helsinki, which had suffered a devastating fire and three Russian occupations before 1810, to be rebuilt on a grand scale, transforming what had been a small town into a magnificent city. To carry out the work he chose Johan Albrekt Ehrenström, a Helsinki-born town planner, and Carl Ludwig Engel, a German architect born and trained in Berlin, who had built St. Petersburg in a neoclassical style.

Between 1813 and 1817, 24 stone buildings and 107 wooden houses were constructed with very strict regulations as to the style of roofs, the size of gardens, and even what color the buildings could be painted (always pastel). The Russian Empire wanted to show the world that it intended to take care of the new, autonomous Duchy of Finland. The centerpiece of the new capital was the Senate Square and the government buildings that surrounded it, along with the white Lutheran Cathedral high above the square. The white cathedral caused Helsinki to be called the White City of the North.

Nicholas Church, Helsinki's Lutheran cathedral, was the last of the many monumental buildings completed during the new capital's Empire stage (1812–1852). Rising above the surrounding buildings, it dominates Senate Square and stands above the harbor with its farmers' market and daily arrivals of international ocean liners. Finnish Tourist Board

Rumblings of Discontent

Though Finland was treated in a very special way as an autonomous grand duchy, there was discontent in the hearts of many Finns. Conflicts over language between Finnish speakers and Swedish speakers persisted. Most of the wealthy and educated were Swedish speakers, and the Finnish-speaking majority found that their language was not taught in school, nor was it used to write the new laws. Judges who understood no Finnish tried cases through interpreters. It was illegal to teach Finnish even in the secondary schools.

The Swedish-speaking upper classes became restless in their bureaucratic positions and felt uncomfortable working under Slavs rather than Scandinavians. Garrisons of Russian soldiers and Russian merchants were common sights in many Finnish towns. Many Swedish speakers moved back to Sweden.

On the other hand, a few Swedes moved to Finland to take advantage of the Russian market. Educated Finns entered the service of Russia in a steady stream, seeking in the imperial realm opportunities to rise to the highest levels of society.

The years from 1809 to 1863 are often called the "period of frozen constitutionalism," since the Diet was not convened and censorship silenced public debate.

Development of a National Identity

Once Finland was separated from Sweden, the question of national identity came sharply to the forefront. Were the Finns now to be Russians? In the first decade under czarist rule, the answer came in a famous statement: "Swedes we are not; Russians we will not be; therefore let us be Finns."

A Finnish nationalist movement began to emerge. Its first advocate was Adolf Ivor Arvidsson (1791–1858), a young journalist who believed passionately that the gap between the people who spoke Finnish and those who spoke Swedish had to be closed. He urged Swedish speakers to make Finnish their mother tongue.

A group of students and instructors at the University of Helsinki, known as the Saturday Circle because they met informally in one another's rooms on Saturday evenings, founded the Society of Finnish Literature in 1831. The group was part of the Romantic Movement that was sweeping Europe and that looked to the common people and the literature of the past as a way of finding national roots. The aim of the Society of Finnish Literature was "to collect the spiritual treasures stored in the minds of the people."

The Power of Language   The Finns' search for a cultural tradition of their own was closely linked with the issue of the Finnish language. Elias Lönnrot (1802–1884) gave Finland its first native literature in the Finnish language when he created a national epic, the *Kalevala*, from old Finnish folk songs. Johan Ludvig Runeberg (1804–1877) became a national patriotic poet. He showed the Swedish-speaking upper classes the virtues of the humble country folk. His *Tales of Ensign Stål* describe the Finnish struggle against Russia in 1808–1809. A favorite poem was of the mentally defective Sven Dura, who "got the command to retreat twisted in his head" and single-handedly held up a whole Russian detachment.

Although Runeberg wrote in Swedish, he created a sense of national identity. A Finnish contemporary wrote, "We recognized ourselves and felt we were one people, that we had a fatherland and were Finns." Another said, "We are Finns, the voice of the poet said in Swedish, and we understood him."

Liberalization under Alexander II (1855–1881)

With the accession of Alexander II in 1855, the Finnish nationalist movement seemed to gain a royal ally. Under the influence of Johan Snellman (1806–1881), who published two important newspapers (one in Swedish and one in Finnish), Czar Alexander II issued the Language Decree of 1863, which recognized Finnish as an official language of administration for the Finnish-speaking population. In gratitude for this decree and other reforms, the statue of Alexander II was erected in Senate Square in 1884, where it still stands, one of the few such statues of a czar to be found outside Russia.

The Language Decree of 1863 has been called the "Magna Carta for the Finnish-speaking part of the nation." It established the important principle of equality, even though Finnish was not in fact spoken in the chambers of the Senate until 1894.

The cause of the Finnish language gained ground. Lönnrot spent eighteen years working on a Finnish dictionary; some educated upper-class Swedish-speaking Finns began to study Finnish and formed a nucleus of a Finnish-speaking cultivated class. Among Finnish peasants religious fundamentalist groups led by people of humble birth arose and created a sense of solidarity. The most celebrated was led by a peasant from Savo named Paavo Ruotsalainen.

Finland Almost Loses Its Autonomy

Within Russia, liberal-minded people were clamoring for reforms. Alexander II hastily drafted a constitution that provided for the establishment of a Russian representative assembly. He had already put his signature to this document but had not yet announced it when he was assassinated in 1881. According to the new constitution, Finland also was supposed to elect representatives to the imperial assembly, which would thus have enacted laws for the grand duchy and eliminated Finland's special status. The Finns did not know for many decades how close they had come to losing their autonomy under "the noblest of Finland's Grand Dukes."

Hints of Russification   Between 1870 and 1890, there were various attempts to limit Finland's autonomy, though none of them succeeded. But the situation did not augur well for Finland. A nationalist movement, Pan-Slavism, was developing in Russia and leading many to ask what Russia was getting out of the relationship with Finland. Finland furnished no conscripts to the army and put a duty on Russian imports. Finland paid no taxes into the imperial treasury (taxes collected in Finland were used within Finland). Adherents of the Pan-Slavic movement started hinting that the time for Russification of Finland had come.

Oppression under the Last Czar   When Nicholas II (1894–1917) ascended the throne, he systematically began to impose a policy of Russification. Russian was made the official language. Finland's own military force was disbanded. Officials who refused to carry out instructions were removed from office. Finnish police and heads of municipalities were replaced by Russians who spoke neither Swedish nor Finnish. Those who defended Finland's rights were exiled to Siberia or shipped to prison in St. Petersburg. A ban on freedom of speech, association, and assembly was imposed.

In 1899 Nicholas II named General Nikolai Bobrikov (1839–1904) governor general. Bobrikov believed the dignity of Russia required that

Finland be Russified at all costs. On February 15, 1899, Nicholas II followed Bobrikov's advice and issued the February Manifesto, placing all Finnish laws under the control of the Russian government. People in and outside Finland were stunned.

THE SECRET PETITION   The Finns drafted a petition asking the Czar to amend the Manifesto. Acting in complete secrecy—the mails and telegraph could not be used for fear the undertaking would be discovered by the Russian authorities—citizens' meetings were held. Signatures to the petition were obtained from every municipality in the country. Students skied across the snowbound land, going from farm to farm and from cottage to cottage to collect names. In less than two weeks, as a result of these heroic efforts, more than half a million signatures were gathered. This included practically all the adult men and women in Finland. Five hundred Finns went in person to St. Petersburg to deliver the petition to the Czar. He refused to receive them. Furthermore, 1,063 scientists, authors, and artists from twelve European countries interceded for Finland. Among them were Thomas Hardy, Florence Nightingale, Anatole France, Henrik Ibsen, and Émile Zola. The Czar refused to receive their petition also.

Russian oppression of Finland intensified. The Finns responded with widespread passive resistance. When Bobrikov asked a Finn how long it would be before all of them were speaking Russian, the Finn replied that it was not an easy question to answer. "You see," he said impassively, "for over six and a half centuries we were closely connected with Sweden, but only ten percent of us speak Swedish."

Finnish children refused to learn Russian in the classrooms. Most Finnish soldiers refused to serve with Russian troops under Russian orders. On June 16, 1904, a young civil servant, Eugene Schauman, shot down the hated Bobrikov and then shot himself. The governor general died the next day. Schauman became a national hero.

A Brief Reprieve   Russia was defeated by Japan in the Russo-Japanese War (1904–1905) the following year, and there were uprisings. A general strike of workers in St. Petersburg spread to Finland. Frightened by the unrest, Nicholas II repealed the February Manifesto on November 4, 1905, thus restoring Finland's constitutional rights. The Diet was reconvened.

The Diet of 1906 made sweeping changes. It established a unicameral Parliament to be elected on the basis of universal suffrage. Finnish men and women of all classes received the right to vote, a right previously held only by the wealthy. Finland became the first region in Europe to grant women the vote. The number of voters increased tenfold, from 126,000 to 1,273,000. In one stroke Finland became the most complete democracy in all of Europe.

Declaration of Independence   On paper Finland had an exemplary democratic Parliament, but if the Czar could dissolve it at will, a step he took four times within its first three years, what good was it? The Czar's determination to impose total Russification remained unabated. By the time World War I broke out, Finland gave the impression of an occupied country, and Russian officials did not consider the Finns loyal enough to call them to arms.

When Czar Nicholas II was overthrown in March 1917, the Finnish Parliament declared that the "supreme authority" that had been vested in the Czar now belonged to itself. The Russian Provisional Government

Not only did Finnish women get the vote in 1906, but in 1907 nineteen women were elected to Parliament—a historic achievement. The thought of women in Parliament stirred fear in the hearts of many. Alexandra Gripenberg (1857–1913), a leading feminist in the first Finnish Parliament, is shown in the photo, and satirized in the cartoon.
National Board of Antiquities of Finland

under Aleksandr Kerensky refused to accept this interpretation and dissolved Parliament.

When the Bolshevik Revolution overthrew the Kerensky government in November, Finland acted quickly. On December 6, 1917, the Finnish Parliament declared Finland's independence.

The First Years of Independence (1917–1937)

At the critical moment when Finland declared its independence, it was not a unified nation. When Parliament announced that it had passed a bill establishing Finland as an independent republic, the political parties in Parliament were so divided that it was not possible to find wording acceptable to all sides. The bill passed by a narrow vote of 100 to 88.

Finland was divided by extreme economic differences between the well-off and the poor in the cities and the countryside, where there were many beggars. The nation was in a state of near anarchy. Violent strikes and mass demonstrations were commonplace. Trade was paralyzed. Unemployment was high. The sudden collapse of Russian fortification projects, which had brought many men to the cities and into close contact with Russian soldiers, threw more people out of work. In the countryside farm laborers struck for better conditions, while tenant farmers feared eviction. Throughout the country, food was very scarce.

Rural Poverty   At the time of independence Finland had about three million inhabitants, of whom 85 percent lived in the countryside. Three quarters of them were poor crofters or landless day laborers. There were more than 60,000 impoverished families of tenant farmers, about 100,000 families of crofters, and more than 200,000 families of landless laborers. A fifth of the rural population was homeless. Whole families could be found living in a small corner of a room in a farmer's home or outside in saunas. Tree bark was used to make bread and coffee, as it had been in earlier hard times.

Armed Bands   Soon the country was divided into two loose military camps. Workers formed quasi-military groups called Red Guards. Farmers in the countryside and property owners in the cities formed Protective Corps, later called White Guards. Finland had no official army and only a weak police force, while Russian troops remained in the country.

Civil War

Seven weeks after declaring independence, the country was thrown into a bitter civil war that lasted four months. On January 24, 1918, after a heated eighteen-hour debate, Parliament called on General C. G. Mannerheim to organize a national force to maintain order and to rid the country of Russian soldiers. The next day the Protective Corps were nationalized. On January 26, P. E. Svinhufvud, the head of the Finnish government, appealed again to the Soviet government to remove its troops and notified the governments of Sweden, Norway, Denmark, France, England, Germany, Austria-Hungary, and Greece of the situation.

On January 27, The Finnish Workers' Executive Committee staged a coup. They took over the government offices in Helsinki and seized control of southern Finland, including the large cities of Turku and Tampere. They declared Finland a Socialist Workers' Republic.

Many members of Parliament fled to Vaasa on the west coast, where General Mannerheim had established his headquarters. Mannerheim, who had had a distinguished career in the Czar's army, moved first against the Russian garrisons in western and northern Finland. About 5,000 Russians were disarmed. By mid-March Mannerheim had enough trained soldiers to attack Tampere, the largest industrial city in Finland and a stronghold of the Reds, who were reinforced by Russian soldiers and supplies.

The Battle for Tampere   The siege of Tampere lasted from March 23 to April 5. It was a bloody battle. The workers fought with ferocious bravery. Women and children fought alongside them. But Mannerheim's better-equipped and -disciplined forces were victorious. Two thousand Reds died and 11,000 were taken prisoner.

With the fall of Tampere, Red resistance broke down in other parts of the country. Soon thereafter a German division landed on the south coast of Finland, invited by Svinhufvud but against the wishes of Mannerheim. Still, many Whites were grateful for German intervention. The Germans took Helsinki. Viipuri in southeastern Finland fell on April 28. The last areas under Red control on the Karelian Isthmus were taken on May 15.

On May 16 General Mannerheim entered the capital with his troops. The Whites had won the civil war. There was cause for rejoicing for many. But both sides had to admit shameful cruelties and unnecessary deaths. Nearly 70,000 Red prisoners, who were starving and cramped into temporary jails, awaited trial.

The Impact of Foreign Powers   The Civil War in Finland was not just a war between brothers. The Soviets supplied arms and assistance

In March 1918 the White forces under General Mannerheim readied themselves outside Tampere for the decisive battle of the Civil War. General Headquarters of the Finnish Defense Forces, Helsinki

to the Reds, and German forces came to the aid of the Whites. Some historians believe that Lenin had expected a socialist Finland to ask to become part of the Soviet Union had the Reds been victorious. Though there were supporters of such a plan, many Finns mistrusted the Soviets. Others, like Svinhufvud, believed that only the Kaiser's Germany could protect Finland's independence.

Almost a Monarchy

The Parliament that met after the Civil War convened without ninety Social Democratic members, who were denied their seats for having supported the Reds. To the surprise and shock of many Finns and foreigners, this Parliament decided in August 1918 that Finland should become a constitutional monarchy—and then in October that the Kaiser's brother-in-law, Prince Fredrik Karl of Hess, was to be king. It never happened. Prince Karl abdicated before he ever stepped on Finnish soil, as Germany collapsed in the last days of World War I.

Svinhufvud resigned two days after the end of World War I, and Mannerheim, who had opposed the pro-German trend in Finland, called for elections.

Finland Becomes a Republic

Parliament reassembled and ratified a new constitution. Finland was to be a republic after all. The author of the constitution, Professor K. J. Ståhlberg, the leader of the Progressive Party, became the first President of the young republic (1919–1925).

The constitution used the old Swedish laws as a foundation, but it also reflected the demands of the monarchists. It gave broad powers to the President, particularly in the conduct of foreign affairs. Of all the European countries that declared their independence after World War I, Finland is the only one whose constitution from that time still remains more or less unchanged.

Treaty with the Soviet Union

Finland quickly gained diplomatic recognition from other countries and settled its borders with the Soviet Union at the Peace Treaty of Tartu in 1920.

Finland received the area of Petsamo in Lapland, which meant the country now extended to the Arctic Ocean. But it gave up its claim to part of East Karelia populated by Karelian Finns, and the Soviets gave up their request for additional territory to protect Leningrad, which was only 19 mi. (32 km.) from the Finnish border. At the time the Soviet government was not strong enough to enforce this claim, but it was not forgotten. Less than twenty years later the issue was raised again by Stalin.

Steps Toward Reconciliation

Many realized that the survival of the nation depended on healing the wounds of the civil war. An amnesty law was passed in December 1919, and 40,000 prisoners were released. Progressive legislation was passed introducing compulsory education, freedom of worship, freedom of speech, and freedom to form voluntary associations.

The critical issue of land reform was handled quickly and well. The Kallio Land Act, named after the leader of the Agrarian Party, Kyösti Kallio, was passed in 1922. Most large farms (over 1,250 acres) sold part of their lands voluntarily to the government at a good price. The government then offered tenants the chance to purchase the land, paying only 7 percent a year until the purchase was complete. Any citizen who did not already own land and who could show evidence of farming skills and who promised to use the land productively also got land. With the comprehensive land reform every third family in Finland gained possession of its own land.

Economic Progress

Immediately after the civil war Finland was on the verge of starvation. Because of the acute shortage of food and medical supplies, 25,000 Finns died during the influenza epidemic of 1918. Mannerheim accepted shiploads of food and a $10-million loan from the United States. Finland repaid the debt and earned a reputation for honesty. (It was the only country in Europe to repay this kind of debt on schedule.)

The country made spectacular progress in agriculture and industry in the two decades after independence. Under the czars Finland had bought most of its wheat from Russia. In 1917 Finland's farmers raised only 6,178 tons of wheat. By 1927 they had increased the yield to 28,954 tons. By 1937, it had grown to 208,511 tons.

Shifts in Politics

Moderate politics and economic growth lessened the impact of the extreme right and left. In 1926–1927 the Social Democrats were allowed for the first time since the civil war to participate in the Cabinet, and the first woman was included. Miina Sillanpää (1866–1952), who had worked to improve the status of working-class women, became the second minister for social affairs. The acceptance of Social Democrats into the government was a great stride on the road to national unity, though it was partly possible because of a widening gap between Social Democrats and Communists.

Many Finns continued to be strongly anti-Communist. The Depression years saw the rise of the Lapua Movement, a right-wing, fascistic faction that carried out kidnappings and staged a march on Helsinki by 12,000 farmers in July 1930. As they got more violent and extreme— even kidnapping former President Ståhlberg—they lost support. After an attempted coup d'état failed in 1932, the Lapua Movement was outlawed.

By 1937 the Social Democrats and the Agrarian Party were able to cooperate on many issues, a sign of increasing social stability. But international tensions would not allow Finland to develop as a neutral Scandinavian country.

The War Years (1939–1945)

As the ominous clouds of World War II gathered, Finland's strategic location on the Baltic again became crucial. A prominent actress, Elli Tompuri (1880–1962), interviewed in Helsinki a few months before the outbreak of war, foretold how the Finns would react if attacked: "We can eat famine bread once more—and survive—start from the ground roots again if necessary. But oppression we can never again endure from any nation—for ours is a rebellious nature."

The Soviet Union and Hitler's Germany signed a nonaggression pact in 1939, but the Russians still feared Germany would attack them through Finland. In October 1939 the Soviet government asked Finland to send a delegation to Moscow to discuss "concrete political matters." Stalin told the Finnish delegation that he needed to improve the security of Leningrad and that this could be done only at the expense of Finland. He explained that Finland's border had to be moved farther away from Leningrad and that the Soviet navy needed a base at Hanko on the southern coast of Finland. Otherwise, Stalin said, Finland could be used as an approach route for an attack on the Soviet Union.

When the Finns asserted that they were neutral, Stalin replied: "I can well understand that you in Finland wish to remain neutral, but I can assure you that this is not possible. The great powers simply will not allow it."

The negotiations were very tense. Finland was willing to give up land near Leningrad but refused to yield a base to the Soviets at Hanko. On November 13 the negotiations in the Kremlin came to an end. On November 30, 1939, Russian planes bombed Helsinki, the Red Army crossed Finland's eastern border, and the Soviet navy approached Finnish islands in the Baltic Sea. General Mannerheim, at age 72, mobilized the Finnish Defense Forces.

The Winter War (1939–1940)

For one hundred days Finland stood at the center of the world's stage as the Finns held out alone against the vastly superior enemy. It was during that time that Winston Churchill said: "Finland alone—in danger of death—superb, sublime Finland shows what free men can do."

Russia's invasion of Finland brought outcries around the world. In New York City Mayor Fiorello LaGuardia formed a committee to sponsor a "Let's Help Finland" mass meeting in Madison Square Garden to raise money. Former President Herbert Hoover organized a Finland Relief Fund, stating that "America has a duty to do its part in the relief of the hideous suffering of the Finnish people." But the goodwill from many parts of the world had little practical consequence. Some Swedish volunteers joined Finnish forces, and very young children were bundled up, tagged, and sent off to Sweden. Many of these children did not return to Finland after World War II, since they had no families to go home to. Still Sweden maintained its neutrality, and when the Allies requested right of transit through Norway and Sweden to aid Finland, their request was rejected.

David and Goliath   The very beginning of the war at the Karelian Isthmus caused a huge traffic jam. As the Russian army with nine divisions poured over the border and shells exploded in the sky, the Finnish army was trying to get to the front while thousands of Finnish refugees with their cows, horses, wagons, sleighs, children, and old folks clogged the roads fleeing to safer areas.

The Russian commander was confident the attack would be over within ten to twelve days and did not bother to issue winter coats for his troops. The Finns were poorly armed and, except for officers, had had little training. However, they knew the woods along their 800-mile (1300-km.) border, and their determination to defend their land gave them stubborn courage. They were also better able to cope with the cold and snow than the lightly dressed Russian troops. The winter of 1939–1940 broke records for its severe cold.

The Russians fought according to the rule books, while the Finns counted on ingenuity. The Russians attacked with large tanks, which got stuck in ditches or could be blown up with Molotov Cocktails. The Finns fought on skis, camouflaged in white uniforms. They would suddenly appear, aim, and then disappear into the whiteness of the winter.

In December, when 20,000 Russian troops advanced across the border north of Lake Ladoga with cannon, tanks, and armored cars in a long column, the Finns encircled them. Soviet planes overhead were not able to attack the Finns without hitting their own troops. For days the Russians were trapped in a five-mile area, and many died after going without food in temperatures of 30° to 40° below zero.

Molotov Cocktails

The Finns did not invent the explosive device of a bottle filled with gasoline. But it was the Finnish soldiers in the Winter War who named it the Molotov Cocktail after the Russian Foreign Minister, V. M. Molotov. Most Finnish soldiers considered him responsible for starting the war.

The Finns had few modern weapons in 1939. They activated ornamental cannons from parks and old hunting rifles. The soldiers also had some submachine guns, but their main weapon against the heavily armed Russians was the Molotov Cocktail thrown with a strong arm and a prayer.

The Finnish army used some 70,000. Soldiers put together 20,000 handmade cocktails at the front lines. The Finnish state liquor board delivered 50,000 regular fifths, already filled with crude kerosene, tar, and gasoline.

The Molotov Cocktail could be deadly, but only if one's aim was sure enough to get into the air-intake holes or open hatches of the Russian tanks.

As deep winter set in, the Russian attack stalled. Stalin was frantic over the news from the Finnish front and rearranged the entire leadership of his armies attacking Finland. This time the Russians stayed out of the forests.

The Russians chose an area where the fields were large and open for their final offensive to break through the Finnish defense lines. By the beginning of February there were twenty-five divisions (600,000 troops) and 440 cannon marshaled against the Finns, who were almost out of ammunition.

Mannerheim had always known that once the Russians prepared a new strategy, they could win by virtue of their superiority in equipment and numbers. The Finns never had more than 300 planes. The Russians flew 2,500 planes over Finnish territory. But it was difficult to prepare the Finnish public for a harsh truce in view of the publicity given the Finnish victories early on.

By February 11 the Finnish front lines had been blasted to bits. On February 16 the Finns began their withdrawal, yet still turned to fight back as they slowly withdrew. At the very last hour of the war the Finns

Reindeer were "drafted" in the north to help carry supplies quietly in their pulkka *(sleds) for the fast-moving ski troops during the winter of 1939–1940.* General Headquarters of the Finnish Defense Forces, Helsinki

still held Viipuri, but the exhausted troops could not maintain their positions much longer. Peace negotiations were already taking place, with the Soviets making new demands for more land. Finland asked again for help through various diplomatic channels, but no aid seemed forthcoming in time. Sweden refused again to jeopardize its neutrality. The Finnish government felt it had no choice but to sue for peace. Finland surrendered on March 6, 1940, and the Peace of Moscow was signed a week later.

Finland had to give up more of its territory than Stalin had originally requested. It lost the southern part of Karelia, where 12 percent of the Finnish people lived. The area made up a tenth of Finland's territory, with important timber and metal industries, and included Lake Ladoga, the Saimaa Canal, and Finland's second largest city, Viipuri. Russia received a thirty-year lease on a naval base in Hanko. Nearly one hundred power stations were turned over to the victorious Soviets.

Finland in Mourning

Flags flew at half mast in Helsinki and all other Finnish cities. Finland mourned its 25,000 dead, its 55,000 wounded, and the harsh terms of the peace treaty. The Finns were given only two weeks to evacuate the 450,000 Karelians who chose to leave rather than stay as part of the Soviet Union.

President Franklin D. Roosevelt expressed the sentiments of the United States in a message sent to both governments on the conclusion of the Treaty of Moscow:

. . . The Finnish nation by incomparable courage and strong resistance against an overwhelming superiority of armaments has won for itself for all time the moral right to live in peace and independence in the land which it has so bravely defended.

But though much of the world had strong sympathy for Finland, it was the policies of Germany and the Soviet Union that were to determine Finland's future.

Uneasy Peace after the Moscow Treaty

Many Finns suspected the Soviet Union still aimed to take over Finland as it had taken over the Baltic states of Estonia, Latvia, and Lithuania. The Soviets' actions did nothing to allay their mistrust. They pressured the Finnish government to remove the Minister of Supply and interfered in the Finnish presidential elections. In December 1940 Molotov announced that if any one of four possible candidates distrusted by Moscow were elected, it would be interpreted as a breach of the peace treaty.

After the German occupation of Denmark and Norway, Petsamo on the Arctic was Finland's only remaining opening to the west. Finland could expect no effective help from Sweden and none from Britain and France. Germany had left Finland to its own devices during the Winter War, but now the situation had changed. Germany was planning a large-scale invasion of the Soviet Union, and it was in its interests to get Finland to fight on the eastern front.

The Impossibility of Neutrality

On September 8, 1940, Finland concluded an agreement with the Soviet Union permitting military shipments to be sent through the southern part of the country to the area leased at Hanko. On September 22 a similar agreement permitting the transport of German soldiers through northern Finland to Norway was signed. The two foreign powers, who were on the verge of war, transported large military units through Finland.

The agreement with Germany turned out to be a point of no return for Finnish policy. The government of Finland repeatedly stated its intention to remain neutral and to normalize relations with the Soviet Union. But by the spring of 1941 Finland's "neutrality" was clearly biased in favor of Germany. The Karelian refugees, whom the country was having great difficulty providing for, still hoped to return to their homes, and rumors of impending conflict between the Soviet Union and Germany encouraged them. Some Finnish officers and politicians unofficially began negotiations with Germany with the intention of mounting a joint military expedition against the Soviet Union.

In June German troops began massing in Lapland. On June 22 Hitler announced that Finnish "comrades in arms" were taking part in an attack on the Soviet Union. Although Finland immediately rejected this claim and declared that it intended to preserve its neutrality, the Soviet Union paid no attention. When German bombers attacked Leningrad, flying over the south coast of Finland en route, the Soviet Union bombed the southern cities of Finland. The Continuation War had begun.

The Continuation War

Finland emphasized it was waging a separate war against the Soviets, fighting for its own ends and not those of Germany. Except for a few extreme rightists in the Patriotic People's League, Finnish leaders were not followers of Hitler's National Socialism. Finland never instituted racial policies, and the small Jewish community of about 1,000 in Helsinki enjoyed full civil rights throughout the war. Finns of Jewish origin fought for their country in 1939–1940 and from 1941 to 1944.

In Finnish history the war is known as the Continuation War, round two of the war that had begun in 1939. The Winter War is regarded as having set in motion the sequence of events leading to the outbreak.

During the Continuation War, Marshal Mannerheim's headquarters was at Mikkeli, from which he made inspection visits to the front. General Headquarters of the Finnish Defense Forces, Helsinki

It has also been called the War of Retribution. There were many in Finland who wanted to go to war against the Soviet Union to regain the territories ceded in the Peace of Moscow.

Stalemate at the Front   In late June of 1941 Finnish troops took up positions on the Soviet border. In July they began to advance, meeting little resistance, and in two months Finnish soldiers had recaptured southern Karelia. Many Karelian refugees returned to their homes to rework their neglected fields and to rebuild their homes. Finnish troops pushed on into Soviet Karelia. But Finland refused to join the German forces in their attempts to advance to Leningrad or to Moscow.

From December 1941 until the great Russian offensive in June 1944, a stalemate existed on the Finnish front. Several times in 1943 and 1944 Finland made gestures for peace. But Germany pressured Finland not to make a separate peace, and Finland was afraid it would be occupied by either Germany or the Soviet Union if it did not keep its army mobilized.

Karelians picked up their belongings three times: first to evacuate at the start of the Winter War in 1939; then to return after Finnish troops reclaimed their lands during the Continuation War; and then in 1944 to leave their homes never to return again. This photo shows their last departure.   General Headquarters of the Finnish Defense Forces, Helsinki

The Soviet Offensive   In the spring of 1944 the Soviets bombed Helsinki. In June they launched their major offensive against Finland under cover of one of the most devastating artillery barrages of World War II. Twenty Soviet infantry divisions and 400 bomber planes advanced against the Finnish lines. The President of Finland resigned on August 1, 1944. Mannerheim, who had been made Finland's only marshal in 1942, was the one leader whom the people would trust not to betray them. He was selected President three days later to undertake the peace talks. Mannerheim did so at once. A cease-fire took place on September 5. On September 19, 1944, Finland and the Soviet Union signed an armistice.

The Terms of Peace   The peace terms were even harsher than those following the Winter War. Finland had to give up even more territory. It lost not only southern Karelia but Petsamo in the north, losing its access to the Arctic Ocean. The loss of territory again brought a huge influx of refugees, as 420,000 Karelians fled back to Finland and Sami left Petsamo. Finland's casualty count for the Winter and Continuation Wars was enormous: 100,000 dead, 220,000 wounded, 50,000 permanently disabled in a country of only 3.7 million inhabitants.

Among the armistice's requirements was the reduction of the Finnish army to peacetime levels. At the same time the Soviet Union required the Finns to expel the 200,000 German soldiers still in the northern part of the country, a force that outnumbered the available Finnish troops. The Germans retaliated with a scorched-earth policy. As they retreated from northern Finland to Norway, they burned towns, villages, and forests behind them. Ninety percent of all buildings in Lapland were destroyed. The Finns called the burned ruins Hitler's Monuments.

The peace treaty also demanded that Finland pay war reparations of $300 million in industrial goods within six years. Some pessimists believed the war damages were so heavy they would reduce the Finnish people to economic slavery. But from the very outset the Finns took the fulfillment of this obligation as a point of honor.

On Finland's Independence Day in 1944, three months after the armistice, the newly chosen Prime Minister Paasikivi told the people:

The path of nations does not rise smoothly upward as we would like to think. Sometimes it leads us to the bottom of a valley that can be as deep as an abyss. . . . The road is hard. We cannot reach the heights without exertion. Great effort is needed. But each step will bring us nearer to the wide horizons.

Developing a Neutral Course

As the actress Elli Tompuri had predicted, Finland had to start from "the ground roots again" after World War II. The country was on the verge of collapse, and the Finns were called upon to demonstrate once again their vaunted *sisu*. Against great odds they found the means to overcome defeat and achieve prosperity.

Every village has its war memorial, and every family has a story of a child sent to Sweden, a relative to the front, or a bomb dropped nearby. There are also stories about Finns forgetting past differences in the united effort to find homes for the Karelian refugees, rebuild Lapland, restore the bombed cities, and meet the harsh demands of the peace treaty.

Finland lost the war but kept its freedom. Apart from Britain and the Soviet Union, it is the only European country involved in World War II that avoided occupation. Had Soviet troops not been needed in the rush to Berlin in the closing days of the war, the Soviet Union might have occupied Finland in July 1944. But Finland's peace cost lives, land, and treasure.

The final peace treaty, signed February 10, 1947, required Finland to surrender a large part of its merchant fleet to the Soviet Union and to make deliveries of various goods including ships and machinery, only 28 percent of which could be its traditional products of wood and paper. A further blow was the requirement that the Soviet Union be allowed to lease the naval base at Porkkala, only 12 mi. (20 km.) from Helsinki.

PORKKALA   The Finnish railway lines between Helsinki and Turku passed through Porkkala. When the Soviets leased the naval base there after World War II, they required that Soviet engines pull the train for this part of the route and that the coaches be covered with iron shutters. It was an offense to try to look outside. Finns referred to this part of the railway line as their "longest tunnel." Porkkala was handed back to Finland in 1956.

Meeting the Reparations

Finland was an agricultural country when the peace treaty was signed. Meeting the war reparations meant restructuring and expanding industry quickly and on a massive scale. The engineering field, particularly shipbuilding, grew at least threefold.

In the autumn of 1952 the last trainload of war reparations left for the Soviet Union. The miracle had been achieved—without help from any other country. (Finland had not accepted Marshall Plan aid from the United States for fear it would be drawn too much into the Western camp and arouse the suspicion of the Soviet Union.) The economic burden had been crushing, but it had set Finland on the path of modernization and created new trade opportunities.

A Russian trawler damaged in the Baltic is being hauled into the Finnish port of Kotka to be repaired in dry dock.   Hannu Vanhanen

The year 1952 was a major turning point for other reasons as well. The Olympic Games were held in Helsinki, Coca-Cola was made available, and Miss Finland was crowned Miss Universe. The Finns began to feel they were on their way to a bright future—and they were right.

Building a New Foreign Policy

At the end of World War II Finland had to recast its foreign policy. Juho Kusti Paasikivi (President of Finland 1946–1956) understood that continuation of a hostile anti-Soviet policy would lead to unending tensions and confrontations. On the other hand, he argued, if the Soviet Union was assured that Finland would not participate in any future attack on the Soviet Union, good neighbor relations could be maintained. He was willing to develop a new direction: a special type of Finnish neutrality to relieve strained relations with the Soviet Union. Finland's approach became known as the Paasikivi-Kekkonen Policy after the two Presidents responsible for its acceptance.

Paasikivi's chances of success were doubted both in Finland and abroad. When asked what he did all day, Paasikivi replied, "I sit, read, and ponder how to keep this country independent—it is a formidable task because one mistake could prove fatal."

Paasikivi was successful, and his approach has promoted peace between Finland and the Soviet Union for over forty years and seems likely to serve as a basis for Finland's foreign policy indefinitely.

(Inset) Paavo Nurmi, the greatest Finnish runner of all time, winning the gold in the marathon at the Antwerp Olympic Games in 1920. Racing shoes were then made of leather. Lehtikuva Oy/Embassy of Finland, Washington, D.C.

Paavo Nurmi bringing the Olympic torch to Helsinki Stadium in 1952. The identity of the final runner carrying the torch had been kept a secret until the last minute, and when Nurmi, then fifty-five years old, entered the Stadium, the audience of 70,000 broke into cheers. Finnish Tourist Board

Friendship Pact with the Soviet Union   In 1948 the Finns and Soviets signed the Finnish-Soviet Pact of Friendship, Cooperation, and Mutual Assistance. This document acknowledges Finland's desire to stand apart from the conflicts of interest of the big powers. In the treaty Finland agreed to maintain a defense force to protect its own borders and to prevent an attack by "Germany or its allies" on the Soviet Union through Finland. If needed Finland would receive assistance from the Soviet Union, but that would be decided separately through consultations. The treaty has been renewed several times during the presidencies of Kekkonen (1956–1981) and Koivisto (1982–) and is now in force until the year 2003.

"Finlandization"   Finland is not a member of NATO nor of the Warsaw Pact. Finnish scholars, diplomats, and ordinary citizens are angered by the term "Finlandization," used in the West to mean passive submission to Soviet domination. Certainly Finland stands in a unique situation as a democratic country sharing a 788-mile border with the Communist superpower. In recognition of the wars in their past, as well as of the fact that Leningrad lies only 80 mi. (134 km.) from the Finnish border, Finnish diplomats have emphasized positive relations and understanding of the Soviets' concern over security. With the Soviet policy of *glasnost*, the term "Finlandization" has taken on a positive meaning. Commentators note that the countries of Eastern Europe hope their relationships with the U.S.S.R. can be similar to that of the Finns.

But there have been tense moments. During the Berlin Wall crisis in the autumn of 1961, the Soviet Union asked for formal consultations based on the Pact of Friendship, Cooperation, and Mutual Assistance. President Urho Kekkonen (1900–1986) suggested an informal visit instead. He had always gotten on well with Khrushchev; the two leaders met quietly on Soviet territory, and the crisis passed without invoking the treaty. The Finns refer to this episode as The Note Crisis.

Finnish politicians and journalists sometimes hold back comments that could be seen as criticisms of the Soviet Union, but they believe this self-censorship is justified by their national interest. When a Soviet missile accidentally landed on Lake Inari in Lapland in January 1986, the incident was handled through quiet and cautious diplomacy rather than with loud public protests. President Mauno Koivisto has said, "In the year 2000 I want Finland to be the type of nation that stays out of the headlines."

Finland in the United Nations and the Nordic Council

Finland is a strong supporter of the U. N., which it joined in 1955. Over 22,000 Finns have participated in U. N. peace-keeping missions, most recently in the Middle East and Africa. The first woman to attain a high post in the U.N. was a Finnish lawyer, Assistant Secretary General Helvi Sipila, who dealt primarily with population control and the status of women (1972–1976).

In 1955 Finland also joined the Nordic Council, which was formed in 1952. The Council does not take official foreign policy positions because Denmark, Iceland, and Norway are members of NATO, Sweden is neutral, and Finland has its own special brand of neutrality. But the Council supports cooperation among the governments of the Scandinavian countries, sponsors cultural exchanges, and permits citizens to travel freely without passports, to work, and to receive public assistance in any of the member countries. Prisoners may even choose whether to serve a sentence in their home country or where convicted. After a residency of two years, a citizen of a Nordic Council country is allowed to vote in local elections, regardless of nationality.

Helsinki: Symbol of
International Relations

During the late 1960's the first Strategic Arms Limitation Talks (SALT) negotiations were held in Helsinki between the United States and the Soviet Union. In 1975 the Conference on Security and Cooperation in Europe led to the Helsinki Accords, creating greater economic cooperation and dedication to human rights. Many said that Finland was the only possible location for such a strategic meeting of representatives from thirty-five nations, because it was the only country in Europe to have the same relations with both West and East Germany, namely, solid trade relations without official diplomatic recognition. In his opening speech to the Conference, President Kekkonen, who had worked for six years to bring these world leaders together, said that true security can be achieved only by "opening gates, not by putting up new fences." His message and actions reaffirmed Finland's neutrality and commitment to good relations among all countries. The Conference put Helsinki on the map and gave Finland recognition as a leader of neutral nations.

Finland's First Socialist President

Power changed hands in Finland suddenly when Kekkonen, who had been President for a quarter of a century, resigned because of illness in October 1981. His successor, Mauno Koivisto (1923–), became Acting President, and then was elected the ninth President of the Republic in January 1982 with an overwhelming majority. He had served as Minister of Finance and as Prime Minister in various coalition governments in 1966–1970 and 1979–1981. As a member of the Social Democratic Party, he is Finland's first socialist President.

His first term as President (1982–1988) saw a period of economic prosperity at home and stability in foreign affairs. Debates at the time of his re-election campaign in 1988 focused more on tax reforms than on political or social crises, though the discrepancy between the country-side and the urban centers is one of Finland's lingering problems. Others are a housing shortage in Helsinki and underemployment of university graduates.

In January 1988 President Koivisto was re-elected for a second six-year term, with 48 percent of the popular vote. He pledged to continue the foreign policies Finland has pursued so successfully since the end of World War II.

President Mauno and Mrs. Tellervo Koivisto attending the sixtieth-anniversary celebration of self-government in the Åland Islands. Mrs. Koivisto has held elected office as a Member of Parliament (1972–1975) and of the Helsinki City Council (1977–1982). Finnish Ministry for Foreign Affairs/Press and Cultural Center

Today Finnish commentators worry less about the shadow of the Soviet Union and talk more of the "Europeanization" of Finland through television, fashions, and travel. "Will Finland still be Finland?" is debated, but this "threat" is too subtle to spoil the enjoyment of the Finns' well-earned peace and prosperity.

Economic Development: "The Mouse That's Roaring"

In 1985 *Forbes Magazine* reported that Finland's $51-billion gross national product ranked it nineteenth in the world, but its $10,440-per-capita gross national product gave it the world's eighth-highest standard of living—ahead of France, number nine, and Japan, number ten. They called Finland "The mouse that's roaring."

The Lure of the Deep: Lauri Rapala was a fisherman earning a difficult living in one of Finland's great lakes, Paijanne. With just a knife, a file, and sandpaper Rapala produced his first wiggling lures, looking like minnows, from pine bark. His catches improved, and it wasn't long before other fishers wanted Rapala's lures. An article in Life *magazine in 1962 led to millions of orders, and though modern technology has taken over the task of carving, each lure is still tested in water and adjusted by hand, piece by piece.* Finnish-American Chamber of Commerce

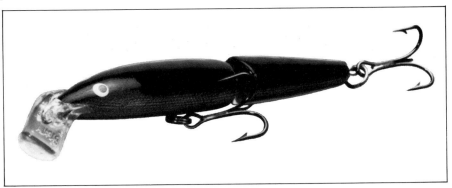

Changes in Basic Occupational Structure, 1910–1985

Percentages of Labor Force

	1910	1930	1950	1960	1970	1980	1985
Agriculture, forestry & fishing	80.0	71.0	46.0	35.5	20.0	12.3	10.6
Industry	12.0	16.0	28.0	31.5	34.0	33.6	31.7*
Commerce	—	—	9.2	13.2	18.8	13.9	21.2**
Transportation	—	—	5.4	6.3	7.1	7.9	7.6
Services	—	—	11.7	13.5	20.0	32.4	28.5
Other and Unknown	8.0	13.0	—	—	—	—	0.3

*includes 7.4% construction.

**includes banks & insurance

Adapted from: Central Statistical Office of Finland and *Statistical Yearbook of Finland 1985-1986*

The prosperity Finland has achieved was hard-earned. From the 1950's to the 1980's the country went through extraordinary changes, and there were serious strikes, debates about farm subsidies, an exodus of skilled workers (300,000 Finns sought higher wages and better housing in Sweden), high taxes, price and wage controls, and devaluation of the finnmark. But in the end Finland can boast of one of the world's best-performing economies. The export of forestry products continues to be important, but metals and engineering are a strong second, followed by chemicals and consumer goods (clothing and footwear, furniture, glassware, and jewelry).

Trading Partner with Both East and West

Finland now has extensive commercial ties with many countries. Its most important trading partners are the Soviet Union, Sweden, Britain, and West Germany, as well as Japan and the United States. During 1987 President Koivisto traveled to India and during 1989 to China to underscore the importance of trade and cultural exchange with Asia.

Balancing East and West

When Finland made a special trade agreement with the Western European Community (EC) in 1973, it also made one with the Eastern Council for Mutual Economic Assistance (CMEA), which includes the Soviet Union, Bulgaria, Czechoslovakia, East Germany, Hungary, Poland, and Romania. Finland's trade with Eastern Europe amounts to 15 to 20 percent of its foreign trade, most of it to the U.S.S.R. Finland and the Soviet Union grant each other special trade rights and try to balance imports and exports. The terms for their trade

Finland's Main Trading Partners, 1987

	Imports		Exports		Trade Balance
	in millions of finnmarks	%	in millions of finnmarks	%	in millions of finnmarks
U.S.S.R.	12,465	14.4	13,522	15.4	+1,057
Federal Republic of Germany	15,125	17.4	9,579	10.9	−5,546
Sweden	11,202	12.9	13,091	14.9	+1,889
United Kingdom	6,183	7.1	9,994	11.4	+3,811
U.S.A.	4,540	5.2	4,524	5.2	− 16
France	3,720	4.3	4,616	5.3	+ 896
Japan	6,136	7.1	1,238	1.4	−4,898
Italy	3,790	4.4	2,243	2.6	−1,547
Norway	1,905	2.2	4,115	4.7	+2,211
Denmark	2,453	2.8	3,407	3.9	+ 954
Netherlands	2,679	3.1	3,141	3.6	+ 462
Belgium	2,239	2.6	1,566	1.8	− 673
Switzerland	1,743	2.0	1,582	1.8	− 161
Austria	1,116	1.3	976	1.1	− 140
Spain	963	1.1	1,119	1.3	+ 155
Other countries	10,418	12.1	12,858	14.7	+2,439
Total imports/ exports	86,677	100	87,571	100	+ 893

From: *Finland in Figures 1988*, Central Statistical Office of Finland.

are spelled out in a "program" that was the first of its kind between the Soviet Union and a free-market economy.

Almost 90 percent of Finland's imports from the Soviet Union are energy products: oil, natural gas, electricity. Finland, on the other hand, exports industrial machinery, ships, consumer goods, and some agricultural and forest products to the Soviets. In recent years 15 percent of Finland's exports consisted of industrial and construction projects on Soviet territory. Finns built one of the newest hotels in Leningrad and a large mining complex and town at Kostamus in Soviet Karelia. The Soviet Union built two of Finland's four nuclear reactors.

Sixty-five to 70 percent of Finland's foreign trade is with Western Europe: the other Nordic countries, the EC, and the European Free Trade Association (EFTA), which Finland joined in 1961. Trade with the United States accounts for 5 to 6 percent.

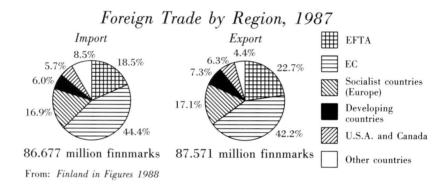

Foreign Trade by Region, 1987

Import

8.5%
5.7%
6.0%
16.9%
18.5%
44.4%

Export

6.3%
7.3%
4.4%
22.7%
17.1%
42.2%

EFTA

EC

Socialist countries (Europe)

Developing countries

U.S.A. and Canada

Other countries

86.677 million finnmarks   87.571 million finnmarks

From: *Finland in Figures 1988*

Finland's balanced trading reflects the country's stated policy of active neutrality. Its Development Aid reflects its humanitarian concern for the less-developed countries. Economic policies aim to strengthen the nation's international competitiveness, curb inflation, and continue to improve employment and maintain high living standards. Domestically, 85 percent of Finland's work force belongs to a trade union, and there are active annual negotiations between unions, political parties, and the Parliament on financial policies. The struggles of the past have helped produce a willingness among Finns to try to negotiate, though with prolonged political debates. Only the future will tell whether prosperity lessens this willingness to cooperate, as some fear it will.

Imports and Exports, 1987

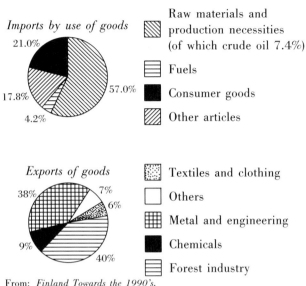

Imports by use of goods
21.0%
17.8%
4.2%
57.0%

Raw materials and
production necessities
(of which crude oil 7.4%)

Fuels

Consumer goods

Other articles

Exports of goods
38%
9%
7%
6%
40%

Textiles and clothing

Others

Metal and engineering

Chemicals

Forest industry

From: *Finland Towards the 1990's,*
The Finnish Foreign Trade Association.

Democratic Traditions

Finland is a constitutional democracy, which balances a strong President, a unicameral Parliament with representatives from many parties, a cabinet of ministers, and a system of independent courts.

The Presidency

Finland is the only Scandinavian country that is not a monarchy, but it has a very powerful President, elected for a six-year term. This office initiates legislation, handles matters of defense, and, most importantly, directs foreign policy. The President may make decisions and sign treaties without even consulting the Prime Minister, Foreign Minister, or Parliament, if necessary. The right to dissolve Parliament, as well as the right to veto a parliamentary bill, is given to the President. If, however, a newly elected Parliament passes the very same bill, it becomes law.

The Parliament (*Eduskunta*)

Parliament has three main tasks: It passes laws, debates and approves the annual budget, and monitors the executive branch (the President, the cabinet, and the ministries) of the country. It consists of 200 members (including one representative from Åland), who are elected every four years, usually with high voter turnout. In recent history there have been four major parties and numerous smaller parties, often short-lived groups that have split off from the major parties.

The President opening a session of Parliament. An electric balloting machine, shown in the right corner of this photo, instantly reveals how the 200 elected members (over 25 percent of them women) vote: On a lit board green signifies "yes," red "no," yellow "abstention," and white "absent." Finnish Ministry for Foreign Affairs/Press and Cultural Center

The Finnish political system clearly tolerates expressions of political difference. The principal parties are the Finnish Social Democratic Party (Soc Dem or SDP), a labor party appealing to workers but distinguishing itself from the Communists; the Center Party (KePu or KESK), formerly the Agrarian Party, representing the interests of people in the countryside and now also trying to form a broad urban base; the National Coalition Party (KOK), a conservative party appealing to business people and professionals; and the Democratic League of the People of Finland (SKDL), a coalition of Socialists and Communists, through which members of the Finnish Communist Party and others run for office.

Since independence no one party has held an absolute majority in Parliament. The four larger parties usually control most of the seats, but they often do not agree on policies so do not vote together. This means that for any one or even two of the major parties to get a proposal through Parliament, they often have to make alliances with smaller parties.

The Swedish People's Party of Finland (RKP), representing the majority of the Swedish-speaking Finns, is one of the original parties in Finland, with about 6 percent of the vote. The Finnish Rural Party (SMP), a populist party dating from the 1960's, still plays a role in opposition politics. The Greens are the largest new coalition (not yet officially a party), holding four seats in the 1987–1991 Parliament; they stress issues of ecology. Candidates have also recently run under the banner of the Christian League of Finland (SKL), the Finnish Pensioners' Party (SEP), the Constitutional Party (POP), the Private Entrepreneurs (SYP), and the Democratic Alternative (DEVA), a Communist splinter from the SKDL.

The parties' strengths are reflected in their memberships on the numerous committees that hold hearings on bills. Parties that do not have members in the cabinet at any given time are considered the Opposition.

Every four years the Parliament elects an Ombudsperson, whose job is to oversee Parliament, the cabinet, and the courts to be sure that the laws are upheld. This position, together with that of the Attorney General (Chancellor of Justice), provides a check on the division of powers among the Parliament, courts, and executive branch. The Ombudsperson is seen as the representative of "the people" should there be complaints against any of these bodies.

The Cabinet

The cabinet, or Council of Ministers (*hallituskunta*), sometimes called the Council of State or even "the Government," is appointed by the President. Unlike the American President, who picks a candidate to head a particular department in terms of his or her qualifications, the Finnish President must also be sure to pick candidates who will represent a balance of political parties so that the total makeup of the cabinet meets the approval of Parliament. Otherwise Parliament can force the cabinet to resign. Cabinet members are usually drawn from two to five parties. It is also possible to have a "caretaker government" of neutral bureaucrats, if a coalition cabinet is not possible.

The cabinet, chaired by the Prime Minister, is the major executive body, producing laws for Parliament to approve or reject. Each cabinet member also heads a government bureau: the Foreign Ministry or the Ministry of Education, of Trade and Industry, of Social Affairs and Health, etc. Once a week the cabinet explains its position on a given matter to the President, who then makes the final decision. When the cabinet resigns, which it often does, it is usually the result of disagree-

ADMINISTRATIVE DIVISIONS OF FINLAND

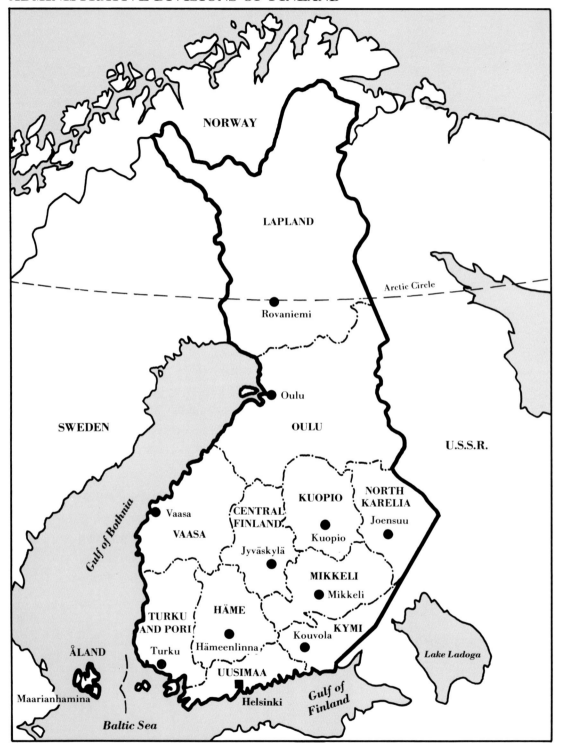

More than 75 percent of Finns over the age of eighteen and eligible to vote do so. During elections the political parties put up posters side by side in specially designated places.
Patricia S. Lander

ments among the various political parties. The President then appoints a new cabinet.

The Prime Minister   By law the Prime Minister has little independent authority, except the power to break a tie vote in the cabinet. He or she does, however, act as the President's deputy during a presidential illness or foreign travel and in reality is an important political leader and social planner. More than half of Finland's Presidents, including Presidents Koivisto and Kekkonen, have been Prime Ministers before their election to the presidency, and speculations about future Presidents usually include the current and former Prime Ministers.

Traditions of Social Concern

Like the other Nordic countries, Finland has striven to create a more just and humane society through legislation. It has a strong system of social security, providing basic health insurance, protection for workers, and pensions. No resident of Finland need fear for the lack of basic necessities. There are special family supports, including maternity leave for ten months (which can be shared with the father), child allowances until the child reaches age seventeen, and free comprehensive school for nine years. Children receive free meals and free dental care at school and transportation to school, and where distances are extreme, as in Lapland, children receive free room and board at the schools. There are special programs for the elderly and the handicapped. This commitment to social welfare has had positive results. Finns are rightfully proud of the fact that they now have one of the lowest infant mortality rates in the world.

Every winter brings out ice sculptors. Angels and castles abound, but there are also contemporary themes. This work portrays the four leading candidates for the office of President in 1988. Patricia S. Lander

The *Talkoot* Spirit

The ethic of social responsibility and mutual help has a long tradition in Finland. The harsh conditions required a pioneer spirit of cooperation. Farmers, for example, banded together to hunt wolves. The custom

Cooperatives

Because the Finns had a strong tradition of cooperating in work, it is not surprising that many Finns were receptive to the idea of more organized and formal cooperatives. The Pellervo Society, named after the god of fertility in the *Kalevala*, was founded in 1899 as a rural nonprofit group for dairy farmers. The Society collected, processed, and marketed the milk that the members produced and then divided the profits among the members.

Cooperative slaughterhouses, meat- and egg-marketing associations, credit associations, and store chains were soon established to return dividends to members at the end of each year.

In 1918 the cooperative movement split between socialists and nonsocialists, Finnish speakers and Swedish speakers, leading to a great many different Finnish cooperative societies.

Even today 98 percent of the milk drunk in Finland is processed through cooperative dairies. Though the majority of large stores are not cooperatives, the cooperative movement played an important role in organizing the Finnish economy. Cooperative banks make 58 percent of the loans to farmers, and cooperative stores sell about 33 percent of consumer goods.

of neighbors working together is called *talkoot*. In the past farmers often helped each other in a project such as clearing a field, putting up a roof, or harvesting the potato crop, and then spent the evening socializing. Sometimes several neighboring families owned tools, large equipment, or bulls jointly. During especially difficult times, the local parish priest or elders would ask farmers to allow the homeless to sleep in barns or saunas.

Women's Rights

The recognition of women's rights came earlier in Finland than in the rest of Europe. Women got the right to vote in 1906 and were the first in the world to run for office. Finnish women have a long tradition of independence. They had major responsibilities on the farms and frequently ran them alone when the men were away in the army or working as lumberjacks. During the period of Russification women shared fully in the protests and strikes.

"Night Courting"   In the countryside young women were given considerable independence growing up through the Scandinavian custom of "night courting." During the summer months a young woman would sleep in a small hut apart from the main farmhouse and might be visited by local young men. There were definite rules of behavior, including songs and verse that a suitor used to try to persuade her to allow him to spend the night. The decision was hers, and there was no stigma if she said yes. It was customary for a couple to be in their mid-twenties and to be expecting a child before they formally married.

Women and Work   When Finland began to industrialize, women left the farms for the cities at a younger age and at a faster rate than men did. Finnish women soon made up a larger percentage of the work

Parliamentary Elections, 1919–1987

Number of Representatives Elected

Party	1919	1939	1966	1975	1979	1983	1987
SDP	80	85	55	54	52	57	56
SKDL	.	.	41	40	35	26	16
DEVA	.	.	.	.	.	.	4
KOK	28	25	26	35	47	44	53
KESK	42	56	49	39	36	38[a]	40
RKP	22	18	12	10	10	10	12
LKP	26	6	9	9	4	.	—
SMP	.	.	1	2	7	17	9
SKL	.	.	—	9	9	3	5
POP	.	.	.	1[b]	—	1	—
The Greens	.	.	.	.	.	.	4
Other	2	10	7	1	—	4	1

SDP   = Social Democratic Party of Finland
SKDL = Democratic League of the People of Finland
DEVA = Democratic Alternative
KOK   = National Coalition Party
KESK = Center Party
RKP   = Swedish People's Party of Finland
LKP   = Liberal Party
SMP   = Finnish Rural Party
SKL   = Christian League of Finland
POP   = Constitutional Party of Finland

In addition, the following smaller parties were represented in the 1975, 1979, 1983, and 1987 parliamentary elections:

STP	= Finnish Labour Party	KVL	= Union of Democracy
SKYP	= Unification Party of the Finnish People	SEP	= Finnish Pensioners' Party
SYP	= Private Entrepreneurs' Party		

In the Parliament elected in 1987, the socialists have 76, the nonsocialists 119, and the others 5 seats.

[a]KESK/LKP = Center Party/Liberal Party.   [b]Constitutional People's Party.

From: *Finland in Figures 1988*, Central Statistical Office of Finland

force than in any other European country. Today they make up 48 percent of the work force and are active in trade unions. Strikes in the late 1970's and 1980's were largely women's strikes: white-collar workers, health-service personnel, and medium-paid civil servants. Women headed four of the major unions in the 1980's.

The majority of Finnish students entering the university today are female. A high percentage of Finland's artists, writers, and architects are women. They constitute 50 percent of the theater directors and are the majority of the new generation of sculptors.

Despite these accomplishments, the goal of equality has not yet been reached. Women earn less than men and work primarily in sex-segregated jobs. While there are day-care facilities, there are not enough to meet the demand, a problem the government acknowledges but has failed to solve. Recognizing the seriousness of these gaps, the Finnish Parliament passed "An Act on Equality between Women and Men" in order to "prevent discrimination on the basis of sex" and "to improve the status of women particularly in working life." The act went into effect on January 1, 1987—eighty years after Finnish women received the vote. Finnish feminists speak of "the unfinished democracy" in Finland, which they are determined to complete.

Literature

Finnish writers and scholars played a decisive part during the country's struggle to attain nationhood. That is one reason why Finns admire them so much and consider the life of an artist or intellectual to be important. Finland has one of the highest literacy rates in the world, and Finns are dedicated readers, following a tradition some date back to the Church Law of 1686, which forbade marriage to anyone who couldn't read.

Books are expensive in Finland. Yet book buying—and using the network of free libraries—is common among the whole population. The Academic Bookstore in Helsinki, designed by architect Alvar Aalto in 1969, is one of the largest bookstores in Europe. But books are sold everywhere in Finland, including the remotest village and quietest railroad station. Popular magazines serialize serious works, and academic dissertations are front-page news in local newspapers.

Folklore and Lönnrot

Elias Lönnrot (1802–1884), one of the central figures in Finnish literature, was born in a small village west of Helsinki of a poor family. He learned to read at home and was sent to school at age twelve. He succeeded in school, got a degree in medicine, and became a country doctor in the remote village of Kajaani, but his real lifework was the collection of Finnish folksongs. Before him, students had recorded the songs of the countryside during their summer vacations, but it was he who decided to create an epic poem from them. He made many journeys (eleven in all) to collect the songs, especially to the Karelian Finns living on either side of the border between Russia and Finland.

The trips were difficult undertakings. Often there were no roads. But Lönnrot had great physical strength, and he excelled in walking, skiing, swimming, rowing, and sleighing. On his first journey he dressed like a peasant with a gun and a knapsack slung over his back, a staff in his hand, a flute in his buttonhole, and a pipe in his mouth. Soon he was taken for a tramp. An innkeeper refused to order a horse for him one day. Another time he left the dinner table of a Lutheran minister and was found writing down an old bath-woman's songs. It is said that at one place the people thought he was a wizard and refused to give him food; he then threatened them with an eclipse of the sun, which was due about that time.

Lönnrot tried to convince anyone he met to sing the songs they knew, which he then copied down. But he made a special effort to seek out the most famous singers, who were called "rune singers," many of whom knew a huge number of poems.

Finland's Epic Poem   Lönnrot edited the songs he collected, putting together themes, characters, and incidents to form a whole, and called it the *Kalevala* (1835). He was only thirty-three years old when this major work was published. He also published a collection of lyric poems, named the *Kanteletar* (*Daughter of the Kantele*) (1840–1841) since folk lyrics were usually sung by women, accompanied by the kantele, a stringed instrument that was plucked by hand.

The *Kalevala* recounts the conflicts between two peoples, the Pohjola in the north and the Kalevala, who live in small groups, separated by great stretches of water, forest, and marshes.

The leader of Kalevala is Väinämöinen, an aged magician who is famous for his wisdom and singing. Other characters are Ilmarinen, the mighty smith; Lemminkainen, a reckless, hotheaded lover who is always getting into trouble; and the tragic Kullervo, who drives his sister to suicide and dies by his own hand. The mistress of the North is Louhi, and her daughter, the Maiden of Pohjola, is so beautiful she is courted by the sun, the moon, the stars—and Väinämöinen.

The world of Kalevala is vast, and the land is full of hostile powers. Objects like iron and wood have the power of speech. Birds and animals are of great importance to the inhabitants of these huge wastes. Fighting plays a smaller part than in other epics. Magic is the great force, and it is used rather than combat whenever possible. As the people of Kalevala rise to overcome their enemies, their trials are identified with the struggles of the Finnish people.

The *Kalevala* had an enormous influence. It has been translated into more than thirty languages, including English. Longfellow read an early German translation and used the meter for his *Song of Hiawatha*. The poem made the Finns aware of the importance of the Finnish language and of the ancient stories of the nation. Its themes have inspired many later artists and musicians. Over three hundred Finnish musical compositions have been based on it.

Early Nationalists

Lönnrot was determined to create a national Finnish culture, as were his friends Johan L. Runeberg (1804–1877) and Zacharius Topelius (1818–1898). Runeberg wrote patriotic poems celebrating the lives of ordinary Finns. His ballad "Our Land" has become the Finnish national anthem. It describes nature and the Finnish countryside rather than war. Runeberg Day, on February 5, is a national holiday, which is celebrated by eating special "Runeberg cakes."

Topelius, the son of an early collector of poetry, lodged in Runeberg's house when he was a student. Though Topelius also became a poet and a journalist, he is best known for his historical novels (*The Surgeon's Stories*, 1851–1866) and his children's books (*Fairy Tales* and *Reading for Children*, 1847–1896). *A Book About Our Country*, an elementary schoolbook, was so popular he came to be called Uncle Topelius.

Runeberg and Topelius fostered a love for the country, but they wrote in Swedish, the language of the minority. It took many years before the first great original work in Finnish appeared: *Seven Brothers* (1870) by Aleksis Kivi (1834–1872).

The Founder of Modern Finnish Literature

The son of a poor village tailor, Aleksis Kivi suffered from poverty, ill health, and depression all his life. He produced all his literary work in

Akseli Gallen-Kallela (1865–1931) is the most famous interpreter of the Kalevala, *which for him was a sacred book. The 1899 painting* Kullervo's Curse *shows the young hero doomed by the feuding of two families.* Finnish Ministry for Foreign Affairs/Press and Cultural Center

less than ten years. He wrote the first tragedy and the first comedy in modern Finnish: *Kullervo* (1864), based on the *Kalevala*, and *The Cobblers in the Heath* (1864), a play about a shoemaker's son's unsuccessful attempts to get married, which is still a favorite with Finnish audiences. But his most important work was the creation of the first novel in the Finnish language.

Seven Brothers tells the story of seven brothers, aged eighteen to twenty-five, who inherit their father's farm when he is killed in a bear hunt. They too like to hunt and expect the farm to produce food for them, but they gradually allow it to go to ruin. Besides that, they find themselves quarreling with the village leaders. None of them can read, and they refuse to learn. When the parish priest threatens to put them in jail, they abandon the farm and escape to "the limitless freedom of the backwoods."

Living in the forest amid nature, they become civilized. When they return to the village nine years later, they agree to learn to read, settle down, and become good farmers and responsible members of the community.

The brothers' qualities—their stubbornness, endurance, and love of liberty—are qualities that the Finns admire and that they have drawn on time and again in the course of their history.

Juhani, the eldest of the brothers, is the most rebellious and quickest to pick a fight. The description of Juhani learning his ABC's after his return is a favorite passage of Finnish readers:

Juhani sat in the cabin, stripped to his shirt and oozing sweat at the table's end, ABC book in hand. Greatly enraged and tearing his hair, he fingered his stout-leaved book. It often happened that, grinding his teeth with rage and almost shedding tears, he would bound up from his stool, snatch the chopping block from its corner, lift it on high, and dash it fiercely to the ground; and at such moments the cabin shook and the man's skimpy shirt fluttered. Thus he would pounce at intervals on the chopping block; for only with much toil did the alphabet take root in the man's head. But he would always sit down again at the table corner and go through a stiff paragraph anew. And at last, as spring came round, he too knew his book from cover to cover; and, with pride in his glance, could close it.

Kivi portrayed the peasants with all their virtues and imperfections. The novel also contained a mixture of styles, and combined humor and realism. When the book was published, the intellectuals in Helsinki said it was a disgrace to Finnish literature. Johan Vilhelm Snellman, the statesman, political philosopher, and great advocate for the Finnish-speaking population, knew better. He alone defended the novel, which is today considered the greatest work in Finnish literature.

The year after it was published, Kivi was placed in a mental asylum. He died the following year at age thirty-eight. His influence and position in Finnish literature have been compared to Mark Twain's in American literature.

MINNA CANTH (1844–1897), THE FIRST GREAT REALIST   Minna Canth's experiences as a wife and widow opened her eyes to society's inequalities, which form the basis of her plays: *A Working Class Wife* (1885), *Children of Misfortune* (1888), and *The Parson's Family* (1891). She was Finland's first major playwright, and her works were powerful inspirations for the workers' and women's movements of the time and still draw audiences today. Since Minna Canth, Finland has produced many women writers. Half of Finland's writers and poets are women.

Basic Themes in Finnish Literature

Finnish literature deals over and over with human beings' relationship to nature. In many novels nature plays a key role as either a friend or an enemy or both. A related motif is loneliness and isolation, which often lead to alcoholism, insanity, or suicide.

The concern for social justice is another important theme in Finnish literature, as is the belief in the worth and dignity of the individual regardless of social status or wealth. Many novels focus on ordinary people, frequently poor backwoods folks. In conflicts between an individual and society, the authors usually side with the outcast or the misfit.

Frans Eemil Sillanpää (1888–1964), the only Finnish writer to win the Nobel Prize for Literature (1939), believed there was a biological basis for human beings' oneness with nature, and many of his novels contain lyrical descriptions of the northern landscape. A Finnish critic said: "Others see nature from man's point of view. He sees man from nature's point of view." His novel *Meek Heritage* (1919) describes a simple cottager caught up in the Civil War of 1918 and destroyed by it.

Mika Waltari (1908–1979), Finland's first internationally known best-selling author, described the middle class and also wrote historical novels such as *The Egyptian* (1945), which was translated into over twenty languages and made into a Hollywood film. Critics now realize that through history Waltari was actually describing his own times and the chaos in Europe after World War II.

Perhaps the best-known novel in Finland is *The Unknown Soldier* (1954) by Väinö Linna (1920–). It has sold more copies than any other work except the Bible, and its characters and sayings have become the common property of all Finns.

Linna was sent to the front during World War II in a machine-gun company. He had come from a very poor family, had left elementary school, and had worked in a textile factory before the war. During the three-year stalemate on the Russian front from December 1941 to June 1944, Linna found an opportunity to read and write for the first time in his life. He turned his own experience into a searing antiwar novel.

The Unknown Soldier gives a realistic picture of war and its cruelties from the point of view of the ordinary soldier. Linna's criticism of the higher-ranking officers led to a national soul-searching and great debate among the whole population that came to be called Finland's Literary Continuation War. At the end of the novel one of the soldiers expresses the feelings of most Finns when he says around the last campfire:

Sosialististen Neuvostotasavaltojen Liitto voitti, mutta hyvänä kakkosena tuli maaliin pieni sisukas Suomi.
The Union of Socialist Soviet Republics won, but spunky little Finland came in a good second.

Another of Linna's important works is the trilogy *Täällä Pohjantähden alla* (*Here Under the North Star*) (1959–1962), which covers seventy years of Finnish history and gives a detailed account of the Civil War of 1918 through the lives of a poor cottager family in a small village.

Modern Finland-Swedish Writers

The first avant-garde writers in Finland and all Scandinavia were the Finland-Swedish poets at the beginning of the century. They inaugurated a rebirth of lyric poetry with the use of free verse and intense imagery. The pioneer of this movement, Edith Södergran (1892–1923) is now recognized as one of the most important poets of the early twentieth century in Europe. She lived, at times in great poverty, with her mother in the family's old summer villa at Raivola in the Karelian isthmus. The villa was destroyed during World War II. Near it the Finland Swedish Authors' Society erected a monument to her in 1960.

The latest author to appear on American bookshelves, better known as a professor of paleontology, Bjørn Kurten provided his own English translation of his fascinating novel about Stone Age life, *Singletusk* (1986).

By far the best-known Finland-Swedish writer abroad is Tove Jansson (1914–). Like *Alice in Wonderland,* her Moomintroll books, translated into twenty-seven languages, can be read on many levels. The Moomins are strange and mysterious but lovable creatures who sleep through the winter and come alive in the spring and summer. For many readers they symbolize the essence of "Finnishness."

Tove Jansson drew the very first Moomin to tease her little brother by drawing the ugliest creature she could. Later the Moomin developed a nicer snout and character. Although the last Moomin book appeared in 1970, new editions are published continually, and Tove Jansson receives over 2,000 letters a year and answers them all individually by hand. Her latest collection of short stories, *Traveling Light*, has characters who may wander far, but the stories are essentially about traveling within oneself. Can one leave old things behind and start anew, traveling light? In this and with her Moomin family she asks universal questions about human nature.

Music, Architecture, and Design

Music

The Finns are great music lovers. There are thousands of amateur musicians, communal orchestras in most towns, and about 1,500 choral societies. Vocal music is an especially strong tradition, because Finland had been a poor country without a wide range of musical instruments. The annual international music festivals—in Helsinki, Pori, and Savonlinna, among others—are always sold out well in advance. Finns from all walks of life and all parts of the country flock to these concerts by the thousands. In the summer alone there are some 1,500 events suited to every musical taste, from jazz and rock to performances on the kantele (the folk instrument, similar to a zither, mentioned in the *Kalevala*) to religious processions such as those of Orthodox Christians at Ilomantsi in eastern Finland.

The Finns have produced so many world-renowned opera singers that some people have wondered half seriously whether "it is the clear air of the north that produces such fine voices." Among these singers are Aino Ackte, the soprano at the beginning of the century who founded the Savonlinna Opera Festival, and singers of the present day such as baritone Tom Krause, bass Martti Talvela, who worked on his farm part of the year in order to be close to nature, and baritone Jormi Hynninen, the son of a lumberjack, who was first exposed to music in church and began to study singing only when he was twenty-five.

One of the World's Great Composers   The Finns are very proud of Jean Sibelius (1865–1957). His seven symphonies as well as the pieces called *Finlandia* (1900) and the *Karelia Suite* (1893) are played by orchestras all over the world. Music scholars today recognize that his work is a continuation of the great symphonic tradition of Beethoven.

Sibelius was inspired, as are ordinary Finns, by a keen sense of nature and Finnish mythology. He drew on the *Kalevala* throughout his life, from the "Kullervo Symphony" (1892), written at the outset of his career, to *Luonnotar* (1913), the strangest and most haunting of his tone poems, which tells the story of the world's creation and which he composed for the opera singer Aino Ackte.

His last work, *Tapiola* (1925), a symphonic poem, evokes the terror of the unending, sunless forests. After *Tapiola*'s completion Sibelius's publisher asked him for an explanation of the title, Tapio being God of the Forest in Finnish mythology, and Sibelius answered with the following quatrain:

> *Widespread they stand, the Northland's dusky forests,*
> *Ancient, mysterious, brooding savage dreams;*
> *Within them dwells the Forest's mighty god,*
> *And wood-sprites in the gloom weave magic secrets.*

Although they were music lovers, the Sibelius family did not approve of Jean's becoming a professional musician, and he enrolled at the Czar Alexander University of Helsinki as a law student. He himself told the story of an uncle, a teacher from the provinces, who visited without warning to see how he was getting on and found a textbook open on his desk. Sibelius describes how he had laid it aside and how, exposed month after month to the air, the open page had become quite yellow. The family gave in, and at the end of the academic year, Sibelius abandoned law for a full-time musical career.

Sibelius was a figure of international importance. Through his work many people first became aware of Finland, a remote province on the northern border of czarist Russia. At the Paris Exhibition in 1900 his music gained attention as the Helsinki City Orchestra played his First Symphony and *Finlandia.* The music seemed to symbolize the Finns' desire to be free from foreign rule. His most famous work, *Finlandia*, became an anthem of the Finnish independence movement. It expressed so much national pride and patriotism that for many years the Russians refused to permit its performance.

Sibelius was held in great affection within and outside his country. His birthdays were national events. On his eighty-fifth, in 1950, the President of Finland drove to his countryside villa to pay the nation's respects.

Sibelius died at age ninety-two. He had been seriously ill in midlife, and his longevity was a surprise. For the last thirty years of his life he was in retirement, living a quiet life with his wife and five daughters in his villa at Järvenpää, 22 mi. (35 km.) from Helsinki. For many his music represents the spirit of Finland, with its classic simplicity, its power, and feeling for nature.

A Surprising Boom in Opera   Musical life in Finland has continued to flourish today. There are many prominent young conductors, the youngest of whom, Esa-Pekka Salonen (1958–), has gained an international reputation and who describes the way he works in characteristically Finnish terms. "My relationship to music," he says, "is like that of a carpenter to wood."

There has been an outpouring of new operas, some commissioned for the annual Opera Festival held in the castle in Savonlinna. Fourteen large-scale works have been produced since 1970, among the most important of which are those of Joonas Kokkonen (1921–) and Aulis Sallinen (1935–). The most popular deal with Finnish history, and evoke the Finns' struggle to be free, spiritually and politically.

Kokkonen's *Last Temptations* (1975) is based on a historical figure, Paavo Ruotsalainen (1777–1852), a poor farmer who became a fundamentalist preacher and exerted a profound influence on Finnish religious life. At the beginning of the opera Paavo is on his deathbed, and in a series of flashbacks he relives episodes from his past life, which has been far from sinless. At the end of the opera Paavo finally attains peace and is set free. All the principal characters are a part of Finland's history, including the academics appearing in one scene who scorned and humiliated Paavo. The opera is immensely popular in Finland.

Sallinen, who is also known as a composer of symphonies, has turned more and more to opera. *The Red Line* (1978) centers on the first election in Finland in 1907. The hero, Topi, a tenant farmer, lives with his wife and children on the verge of starvation and hopes that voting for the Reds, the socialists, will relieve their plight. But change is too slow to help them. When Topi finally meets the bear that has been killing his sheep, the bear overpowers him. The title refers both to the

The castle courtyard at Savonlinna is transformed into an opera stage during the annual summer festival. Olavinlinna (the Castle of St. Olof) was begun in 1475 to protect lands disputed with Russia.   Hannu Vanhanen

mark that the people make on their ballots and to Topi's blood that streaks the snow at the end. Another of Sallinen's operas, *The King Goes Forth to France* (1984) is a strange tale of power politics set in a future Ice Age.

The upsurge in opera has led one music critic in Helsinki to exclaim, "Finns used to be proud of their sportsmen. Now they have turned to opera composers!"

Architecture

Inspired by nature, Finnish architects have stressed the importance of creating harmony between a building and its surroundings. They are known for integrated designs that pay attention to everything from the town plan to the shape of buildings, to the interiors and furniture— including even doorknobs.

Ordinary Finnish citizens notice and comment on architecture. Old stone churches or very modern ones are studied and debated. A railroad station or government building, a school or museum, stately brick factories beside waterfalls, a new library—all contribute to a Finn's evaluation of an area.

The Saarinens   The massive granite railroad station in the center of Helsinki designed by Eliel Saarinen (1873–1950), and built between 1906 and 1914, is considered one of the best and most imposing railroad stations in Europe. Eliel Saarinen had two careers: one in Finland and one in the United States. He moved to the U.S. after winning second place in a design competition for the Chicago Tribune Building (1923), which set the standard for American skyscrapers of the 1920's and 1930's.

When historians of architecture discuss Eliel and his son, Eero, they note their Finnish contribution to American "modernism": the idea that function need not be distant or cold but must respond to human use and scale. Eero Saarinen (1909–1961) designed, among many other works, the TWA terminal at New York's Kennedy Airport. It looks like a giant prehistoric bird about to fly.

Alvar Aalto   The best-known Finnish architect is Alvar Aalto (1898–1976), whose influence covered broad areas: regional and urban planning; designs for homes, churches, and larger buildings; but also interior decoration (textiles, furniture, glass vases, lighting) and industrial art. Before he gained recognition as an architect, Aalto's furniture won awards in the 1930's. His early chairs were made out of bent and glued birch plywood. One of his popular vases imitates the outlines of a Finnish lake in its irregular shape. Aalto's creed was similar to Saarinen's: "One must go down to the source of all things: to nature."

Aalto believed the Finnish environment was challenging enough without adding to the stress. His idea was that the human-made environment should provide the nourishing surroundings denied by nature during most of the year. His libraries, churches, university, and administrative buildings are functional but also expansive, including undulating curves of wood or brick, and stairs and views reminiscent of Italian hill towns, of which he was fond. Wherever possible Aalto created links back to the forest, which he considered Finland's prime physical and emotional resource.

Spouses and Partners: Aino Marsio Aalto, Raili Pietilä, and Loja Saarinen   The first professional women architects in the world were Finns. Aino Marsio Aalto (1898–1949) and Raili Paate-lainen Pietilä are two examples. Some scholars have argued that the way Aino Marsio and Alvar Aalto complemented each other was the key to

Finlandia House, designed by Alvar Aalto (1971), has become the symbol of Finland's international role. It complements the nearby Parliament House (1921, J. E. Siren) to the left and contrasts with the National Museum (1912, Saarinen), whose tower is visible to the right. Finnish Tourist Board

NATIONAL NEEDS   Aalto was called on to design industrial plants and homes for workers and for refugees. His plans for rebuilding entire cities like Rovaniemi, Oulu, Säynätsalo—projects demanded by war devastation—made Aalto into Finland's "national architect." His last great work, Finlandia House in Helsinki (1971), one of Europe's finest meeting centers, is a monumental work in white marble. It was here the Helsinki Accords were signed. Aalto designed every inch, down to the last ashtray.

Alvar Aalto's success. Aino Marsio Aalto was seen as the social con-
science and the one who followed through with the design after Alvar
Aalto's initial sketches. She was also known for her artistic breakthroughs in etching glass in the 1930's.

Architect Raili Pietilä works with her husband, Raimo Pietilä, on
many projects ranging from churches and town centers to the new
presidential residence. Loja Saarinen, the second wife of Eliel Saarinen,
was a gifted sculptor, textile designer, and weaver, who frequently
contributed to his plans.

*The public library in Tampere, opened in August 1986, was designed by the Pietiläs in
the form of a golden-brown grouse, a game bird common in the Finnish countryside.
Construction of the library required innovative techniques for shaping the concrete, copper,
and granite to fit the unusual design.* Hannu Vanhanen

The Finnish pavilion at the Paris Exhibition in 1900 was designed by the young partnership of Eliel Saarinen, Armas Lindgren, and Herman Gesellius, who worked together from 1897 to 1905. It was acclaimed as an extraordinary merger of Finnish national romantic themes with the international art nouveau style. The music of Sibelius, the architecture of Saarinen, and the paintings of Gallen-Kallela drew crucial attention to Finland at the peak of Russian oppression. National Board of Antiquities of Finland

MASS PRODUCTIONS   In the 1960's and 1970's there was so much building activity using prefabricated units that what had once been seen as esthetic simplicity turned into faceless uniformity. In reaction to the mediocre mass productions, attempts were made in the 1980's to restore historical houses and areas in cities where possible and to stress again a closeness to nature and the human element.

New Directions   The most radical departure from Aalto is seen in the work of Raimo (1923–) and Raili (1926–) Pietilä, who were chosen to design a new residence for the President of Finland in 1987. They have been described as anarchist, unconventional, expressionistic architects, reflecting a search for new ideas.

Design

The Milan Generation   Just as Finland was first noticed at the Paris World Exhibition in 1900, a breakthrough for Finnish design came in the Milan Trienniale, an international art exhibition in Milan, Italy, in 1951. Finland won more honors than any other country, and the Trienniale winners were celebrated like Olympic heroes. Finland's reputation as a leading design country was made almost overnight. Tapio Wirkkala (sculptor and glass designer, known for his iceberg designs), Kaj Franck (known for textiles, mass-produced ceramics, and glass), and Timo Sarpaneva (known for graphic design, ceramics, and glass) gained international reputations. The American magazine *House Beautiful* chose Tapio Wirkkala's wooden bowl as the most beautiful object in the world in 1951 and later chose Timo Sarpaneva's glass sculpture.

Modern Finnish design is simple without being austere and useful without being cold. Each crafted piece is functional but also a work of art. A glass vase is shaped so that it will be beautiful as a container for summer flowers but also as an object that can stand empty in winter like a sculpture.

By the 1960's Finnish design had specialized in the "first-rate everyday object." The materials are the basic elements of Finland: wood, fur, cloth, clay, and granite.

Much of the design of the 1950's and 1960's is still popular, and many of the designers are still active. The 1970's and 1980's, however,

Glass is a favored medium for Finnish designers, including the noted artists Timo Sarpaneva (glass sculpture), Kaj Franck (woodcock), and Tapio Wirkkala (vase). The chair is by Yrjö Kukkapuro, a leading name in interior design. Finnish Ministry for Foreign Affairs / Finnish Tourist Board

Materials and Crafts

Ceramics: In ceramics the Arabia company (founded in 1874) has been a well-known producer of hand-painted dishes for decades, as well as simple, solid, reasonably priced sets. The factory now has a few robots to take the large hot bowls in and out of the oven, but the hand-painting and careful checking continue.

Fabric: One of the most stimulating expressions of Finnish artistry has been in its informal, bold and challenging clothes, first pioneered by Armi Ratia, founder of Marimekko, whose wild, big prints and simple styles suggested a style of living as well as fashion in her fabrics, dresses, blouses, and capes. This tradition has been expanded by Vuokko Eskolin and Marjatta Metsovaara.

Wood: The classical saunas (and wooden buckets and benches) and birch furniture are still in demand, but there is also wooden jewelry of all colors and designs, wooden Christmas decorations, carvings of sheep, bowls and plates, utensils, children's furniture and toys. Currently, slim furniture designed with enameled steel tubes and birch plywood is on the market.

Sculpture: There are sculptured figures everywhere in Finnish towns. An outstanding creator of Finnish public sculpture was Wäinö Aaltonen (1894–1966), who not only used marble, ceramic, and bronze but was the first modern sculptor to use granite. His many statues include one of Paavo Nurmi running (1924). Finland has many women sculptors today. Eila Hiltunen (1922–), who specializes in welding techniques using bronze and copper, constructed the twenty-four-ton Sibelius monument in Helsinki from 1963 to 1967.

brought some counterreactions. The Milan Trienniale in 1966 was closed by demonstrations. The student radicalism of the 1960's protested the "star system" and "object worship," which they said prizes promoted, and within Finland Kaj Franck, one of the greatest stars of the golden era of Finnish design, became artistic director of the Helsinki University of Industrial Design and demanded anonymity in design.

Finnish Industrial Design   Many Finnish designers create both for industry and the home. The difference between art and design, and between different mediums, is constantly blurred. A silversmith designs cutlery; a glassblower designs tools and utensils.

The first certified industrial designers graduated from the University of Industrial Design in 1961 and have designed radiotelephones, computers, rowing machines, icebreakers, and forestry and mining equipment. As important as trained designers are, the single most successful Finnish export item of all time was created fifty years ago when Lauri Rapala, a professional fisherman, carved a lure from a piece of pine bark.

Yrjö Sotamaa, the Rector of the University of Industrial Design still emphasizes that the starting point for any design is "the elements of nature—fish, reeds, grasshoppers, the golden gleam of water, the meandering shorelines of the archipelago." But the younger generation is pushing past functionalism and looking for a new identity. In an 1988 interview, the Rector summed up:

The history of Finnish design is one of vacillation between two worlds—the East and the West—and the two worlds of value associated with them. One extreme is provided by a strict functionalism based on the puritanism of Lutheran ethics. Everything which is not directly linked to the intended use of the object, its utility, is a Bad Thing. The other extreme is provided by the Byzantine tradition of the

The Finnish Ryijy Rug

The tradition of weaving ryijy rugs dates back to the fourteenth and fifteenth centuries. They were used as bedcovers during the winter, as traveling rugs on boats or on sleighs, or hung on walls to keep out drafts.

The first ryijy (in Swedish *rya*) were created to look like animal furs. The advantage of wool over fur was that it would dry much faster. In western Finland and the Åland Islands rjiyj rugs were collected as taxes. By the eighteenth century some wealthier farmers began to view them as decorative art and hung them on walls. They were passed down from one generation to another and were sometimes used during weddings as ceremonial carpets.

The classic ryijy is partly woven, partly knotted by hand, on a loom. To make the rug soft, the tufts are one and a half to two and a half inches long. The traditional ryijy was made of undyed wool, using the natural black, gray, or white color of the sheep. Today ryijy wool comes in 160 shades, and frequently two or three different colors are tied in one knot to achieve the intensely bright effect for which Finnish ryijys are famous. A ryijy may have up to 100 different shades, which is why they are sometimes described as poems of color.

The modern ryijy is an example of applied arts. The traditional form was revived in the 1950's, after a decline in the mid-nineteenth century, through the efforts of the Friends of Finnish Handicraft (founded in 1879) and Neovius (founded in 1889). The modern ryijy is almost always based on abstract or geometric patterns, whereas earlier rugs often had tulip, star, or tree-of-life motifs.

East. The abundance of forms, the richness of decorative elements, and the melancholy poetry are traces of the Byzantine in Finnish design. The gleam of gold, radiance, and lyricism are to be found in an increasing number of works representing contemporary Finnish design. We are on the way to Byzantium.

Finland's outpost position as a bridge between East and West allows for an exchange or an alternation of influences. Since the West has made such an important impact recently, Sotamaa predicts the pendulum will swing to the East. Not everyone agrees, though all know that the basic images of Finnish design reflecting nature will remain, regardless of the style.

CHAPTER XVI

Holidays and Special Occasions

Pre-Christian folk traditions blend with customs from Sweden, Russia, and Germany to create a number of high points in the Finnish year. There are Christmas and New Year celebrations in winter, *Vappu* in spring, and Midsummer in June. National holidays such as Independence Day (December 6), Kalevala Day (February 28), and Runeberg Day (February 5) are also observed. Older special days associated with the agricultural cycle, such as "driving-out day," when cattle were taken to the fields, or St. Erik's Day, when the last of the migratory birds were expected back in May, are now hardly noted. But old saint's days have been changed into "name days," an interesting custom giving everyone a second birthday.

Christmas

Christmas is the most important holiday of the year, coming after the long, dark autumn. At noon on December 24, church bells proclaim the "peace of Christmas," and all secular activities stop. The celebration lasts three days and is preceded by a lengthy period of preparation, including Christmas bazaars, decoration-making parties, and then *Pikkujoulu* (literally "Little Christmas") parties. These small parties are held the week before or after December 13, one of the shortest and darkest days of the year (known as St. Lucia's Day in Swedish areas).

Christmas is a festival of light, illuminating the dark winter. A favorite Finnish carol begins, "Oh, has summer come in the midst of winter?" Lighted candles are placed on the Christmas tree and in windows of houses, an old custom to encourage churchgoers. In the past people from villages sometimes had to drive for hours by sleigh to reach the church door, but their way was brightened by candles in houses along the roadside.

Finnish cemeteries are ablaze with light. At sunset on Christmas Eve families make their way to the churchyards and place candles, called "fires of life" from an Orthodox tradition, on the graves of loved ones.

The Christmas Eve sauna is followed by the Christmas meal of fish, ham, and rice pudding. In the countryside farm animals and birds are given extra food. In the city oats are put out in special feeders for birds.

In earlier times Christmas celebrations were like pre-Christian harvest festivals, transferred from early November to December. Traces of these older Scandinavian festivals remain in some Finnish Christmas decorations, like the straw goat figurines and the *himmeli* (heaven), a large mobile made of straw, which hangs above the Christmas table. The straw goat led the harvest processions. The word for the Finnish Santa

Claus retains the old association—he is called *Joulupukki*, literally "Christmas goat."

A Finnish broadcaster of a children's radio program announced in 1927 that Joulupukki lived on a mountain called Korvatunturi in eastern Lapland. This idea caught on. The Finnish government and the Finnish Tourist Board have created a Santa Claus Land at the Arctic Circle. Joulupukki now looks much like the American Santa Claus, with a workshop in Lapland near Rovaniemi, special elves and reindeer, and a special post office that replies to 200,000 cards and letters (120,000 of which come from abroad) every year.

New Year's Eve

Finns, Hungarians, and other Europeans often start the New Year by pouring lead to predict the future. A small block of lead is melted, thrown into a bucket of cold water to harden, and then "read": Bulging bubbles mean money; black spots mean future sadness. Travel is predicted if the shape looks like a boat.

May Day (*Vappu*)

The first of May (*Vappu*) has a special meaning for everyone in Finland, but which meaning the Finns celebrate depends on their political outlook.

Celebrating Spring   May Day, which was once a pagan festival to welcome the spring, is marked by a carnival-like atmosphere with balloons, streamers, horns, and masks, and the wearing of new, light-colored spring clothing—even if it snows. There are concerts, fairs, and parties where special home-brewed drinks made of lemons and raisins are consumed as if they were champagne.

At graduation high school students receive white caps that symbolize their success. These caps are worn on festive occasions throughout one's life, but especially at Vappu.   Hannu Vanhanen

Student Day   On the evening before May Day, students gather to enjoy themselves. In Helsinki they all meet at a fountain of a mermaid near the harbor and a student climbs the statue at midnight to place a student cap—white with a black peak—on her head. The festivities continue the next day with student processions and more partying.

Labor Day   Socialists have adopted May Day as Labor Day (as it is in most European countries, East and West), and they set a serious tone for *Vappu* morning with parades and speeches. Throughout the country factories that "never close" are closed on two days of the year: Christmas and May 1.

Few Finns today think of Finland as divided between socialists and bourgeoisie, Reds and Whites, or workers and capitalists, as they did during the early days of the Republic. *Vappu* is one of the few expressions of this old division: the workers with their parades and speeches in one part of town and the students (seen as bourgeoisie) in another. Each group considers it an important day, and for those who fall into neither socialist nor student camp, it is still a great day to celebrate the coming of spring.

Midsummer (*Juhannus*)

Juhannus (Midsummer) is another festival of light, celebrating the summer solstice, when the day is at its longest. Thousands of bonfires (earthly suns) are lit. In earlier days the bonfire was observed for revelations concerning the future, and it was believed that spirits and ghosts made their own little fires to clean treasures on Midsummer Eve.

Various customs date to pre-Christian forms of magic used to ensure a plentiful harvest and fertility in the coming year. Houses, boats, buses, and large buildings are covered with fresh birch branches. On the Åland

Municipalities, clubs, neighbors, or families may build their own bonfires along the shore of the Baltic, a lake, or a river at Midsummer. Finnish Tourist Board

Islands, tall poles are decorated with flowers and leaves. Midsummer supper tables are adorned with birch and garlands of flowers.

Midsummer night was particularly associated with love magic. A young girl who had gathered nine different herbs and placed them under her pillow believed she would see her future husband in her sleep. Many other forms of predicting a spouse were practiced at Midsummer, and some of these are kept alive for entertainment and fun. Around the bonfires national costumes from different regions are sometimes worn and traditional folk dances are performed.

The Church made the pagan festival into St. John's Day, the Saturday closest to the summer solstice, and the Finnish government has made it flag day. In the past, most marriages took place after the fall harvest, when food was more plentiful, but nowadays weddings at Midsummer have become quite popular.

Flowers and Coffee

Just as surely as Finns celebrate Little Christmas, they make a special occasion of drinking coffee: afternoon coffee, evening coffee, church coffee, name-day coffee, sauna coffee, engagement coffee, funeral coffee, and so forth. Finns consume more coffee per person than any other people in the world. Drinking coffee is not a casual cup from a takeout counter, as in the United States. Coffee requires sitting down, preferably with a neighbor, colleague, or friend, and making a pause in the pace of the day. Some scholars compare the ritual of a Finnish coffee to the Japanese tea ceremony. A simple coffee includes a slice of *pulla* (a Finnish sweet yeast bread), but coffee for visitors starts with something salty (Karelian rice *piiraka*, open-faced sandwiches, or slices of cheese), and may include a *pulla* ring or buns, two or three types of cookies and spice cake, and ends with a final round of whipped-cream cake.

On the table near the coffee cups there is frequently a bouquet of flowers. In a country where the growing season for flowers is short, every blossom is cherished. Finns taking a walk in May check whether the early anemones are opening and in the fall watch the last flowers. Flower shops stock flowers all year round, and the proper guest arrives with flowers—always an odd number, so even one flower is acceptable—often bought at the nearest train or bus station. At graduation a gift of roses is required, while wild flowers picked on the way to visit a friend would be flowers enough for a casual occasion. This is just another way in which Finns renew their ties with nature.

National Dress

In the 1880's students and intellectuals in Helsinki were concerned at the loss of examples of traditional costumes worn by the rural farming population for festive occasions in the eighteenth and nineteenth centuries and began to collect them. The basic woman's dress consists of a long skirt, white blouse, vest, and cap, with many local and regional variations. Men wore tight knee breeches in the eighteenth century and long trousers thereafter, with a colorful waistcoat and a white full-sleeved shirt with stand-up collar.

National costumes have become popular for festive occasions. There have been so many questions concerning the "correctness" of shoes, jewelry, etc., that in 1979 The Finnish National Dress Council was formed to promote research and give advice connected with national costumes. There are also several craft schools that teach how these costumes were made traditionally.

Sports

Finns love to run, ski, and participate in other sports. The victories of Finland's athletes, coming at key moments, strengthened the Finns' sense of national pride and made the rest of the world take notice.

During the years when Finland was struggling to maintain its liberty against the czar, the Finns gained important victories at the Olympics. At the Olympic Games in Stockholm in 1912, nobody could ignore the Finns. They staged a political protest at the opening ceremonies by marching under their own standard, apart from the Russian team, to demonstrate their status as a separate nation. Then they made their presence felt by winning twenty-six medals, including nine gold. In a particularly dramatic race, Hannes Kolehmainen won the 5,000-meter race, defeating the great French runner Jean Bouin in a legendary final spurt. The Finns call his victory "Finland's great overture." The next decade was to bring even greater victories.

National Heroes

The recognition Finland received through its long-distance runners was particularly important immediately after the country declared its independence. Paavo Nurmi, "the Flying Finn," was the most famous Finnish athlete of all time. He was said to have *run* Finland onto the map of the world by winning nine Olympic gold medals from 1920 to 1928. The Amsterdam Olympics in 1928 came to a climax in the 10,000-meter race with a battle between Paavo Nurmi and Ville Ritola, another great Finnish runner, who won five gold medals in his career. The two Finns dominated the race, and after a fierce struggle, Nurmi finally took the lead and left Ritola behind in the stretch.

In the 1970's another Finnish runner, Lasse Virén, won both the 5,000- and 10,000-meter races in the 1972 and 1976 Olympics. Nurmi and Virén are national heroes in Finland.

Finland has won many Olympic medals in its "traditional" sports— long-distance running, wrestling, javelin throwing, and above all, recently in skiing. But Finland has also moved ahead in newer fields like motor sports. Nowadays its most famous international stars are rally drivers like Keke Rosberg, the retired world champion Formula One driver, who is probably one of the best-known Finns in the world today.

From 1971 through 1986 out of 147 official world championship rallies, Finnish drivers won fifty-six of them. The drivers of Sweden and France each have captured twenty-eight world championships for their countries—that is, half as many as the Finns have won. Rallycross, which combines elements of rally and race-track driving, is yet another new motor sport in which the Finns do well.

When asked to explain why they have produced so many great drivers, the Finns usually talk about their long-distance runners and their fierce spirit of independence. Markku Alen, one of the best rally drivers, has said:

We Finns have never been brilliant team players. Just look at how we play soccer. But we shine in those sports which demand courage and the ability to make independent decisions. That's how Lasse Virén, Paavo Nurmi, and many others have succeeded in grueling long-distance running. That's also the way that we struggle by ourselves in rallies against the clock. Finns don't want to lose!

Games and Sports in Daily Life

The Finns have been called a "sports-mad population." No matter where a Finn may be, he or she is not far from sports. Even in the middle of a crowded city, there are networks of bicycle paths leading to nearby forests where one can pick a short or long trail for hiking, biking, or cross-country skiing, depending on the season. In summer there are track and field events and soccer. In winter there is skiing, ski jumping, and skating.

With increasing prosperity, more and more Finns have leisure time for sports. Skiing is the national pastime. Today Finns ski for enjoyment. In the past, before transportation and communication improved, it was necessary to be able to ski to get from one village to another in winter.

The Finns especially enjoy cross-country skiing and ski jumping. Many villages and almost all towns have their own ski jumps, and there are more than 200 of them in Finland. During the long winter on weekends and after office hours, thousands of people of all ages, from the very young to old pensioners, can be seen skiing along well-lit trails in the forests. A week-long ski vacation is built into the school year. Every Sunday long cross-country ski trips are organized. The biggest is the Finlandia Ski, which begins in the city of Hämeenlinna and ends in Lahti 45 mi. (75 km.) away. It is the biggest keep-fit event in the country.

Finnish children enjoy all sorts of winter sports. They learn to sled on pieces of plastic shaped like big Frisbees, just the right size for two-year-olds to sit on. During the school day there are a great many

Finns learn to ski almost as soon as they learn to walk. Toddlers are taught on specially made trainer skis. Schoolchildren ski regularly and look forward to learning to jump.
Finnish Tourist Board

breaks for sports and exercise. Every forty-five minutes of class is followed by a fifteen-minute recess. The Finns' educational philsophy is that physical exercise is good for the mind as well as the body. They believe the children will return to the classroom better able to study and concentrate after vigorous exercise.

Aerial view showing 14,000 cross-country skiers setting off at the starting line of the annual Finlandia Ski Race in Hämeenlinna. Participants represent more than twenty-five different countries, including the U.S. and Canada.   Finnish Tourist Board

Finns play a type of baseball called *pesäpallo*, which they consider their national game. It is played from an early age by both girls and boys. Finns explain that *pesäpallo* is good endurance training for life and for war, where the effort needed to make the next goal always seems to increase.

School children also learn important skills in orienteering, a game of pathfinding through the wilderness.

In the last twenty years, new sports facilities have been built in all parts of the country. Most municipalities have indoor pools for year-round swimming, ice hockey rinks, downhill slopes, gymnasiums, and soccer fields, which are open to everyone. About one in four Finnish

Orienteering

The game of pathfinding through the wilderness is very popular in Finland. The object is to reach a certain known objective miles away in the shortest time, armed only with a compass, a map, and some food.

The sport makes a person at home with unknown regions of the country. It requires stamina, speed, and sharp wits—qualities that helped the Finns ward off an enemy fifty times their size in the Winter War of 1939.

The Finnish Civil Guard was untrained, but they were able to keep the Russians off guard because they were expert skiers who could maintain their orientation in the forests and quickly find their targets.

In contrast to American baseball, in Finnish pesäpallo *the distance between the bases increases as the player progresses around the field, so it is a longer run from second to third than from first to second, and an even longer run to home.* Hannu Vanhanen

citizens ten to seventy years of age belongs to a local sports club affiliated with the nationwide sports organizations, the Finnish Sports League (SUL) or the Workers Sports League (TUL).

Finland no longer needs victories in international sports to remind the world that it exists or that Finns can persevere. But sports are perhaps an even more important part of daily life than in the past, especially for those who live in cities and want to keep in touch with nature, which is a basic need for Finns.

Ice hockey, a favorite game, is one of the most popular spectator sports. Finnish players such as Jari Kurri, Ilkka Sinisalo, and Esa Tikkanen have gone on to star in North America's National Hockey League. Hannu Vanhanen

Toward the Twenty-first Century

As Finns look ahead to the twenty-first century, most agree that their lives are easier than their parents'. By the 1960's the words "Poor we shall always remain" in the national anthem had been proved wrong for the first time since they were written in 1846. Dag Hammarskjöld (1905–1961) of Sweden, Secretary-General of the U.N. from 1953 to 1961, used to say that to be born in Scandinavia was like receiving a winning ticket in life's lottery. Nowadays Finns feel the slogan applies equally to them. There is no longer the feeling of being Sweden's poor stepchild.

Finland's survival as an independent nation is now taken for granted. The country is often described as a great exception. It is the only European country that gained independence after World War I that has maintained its constitution and economic system through World War II and its aftermath. Most Finns have great sympathy for citizens in the Baltic states of Estonia, Latvia, and Lithuania, who are trying to reassert their national identity and push for more independence within the Soviet system. Many observers had expected Finland to be in the same position as its neighbors across the Baltic.

Finland worked hard to turn its location between East and West into an advantage rather than a liability. It has kept ties with both blocs and has used the Soviet marketplace well—to export goods to the U.S.S.R. that might not be as competitive in the West, and to import needed fuel from the U.S.S.R.

Nuclear Chessboard

There are always lingering problems, especially since the Arctic zone has become more strategic and important militarily. The Arctic has been called the nuclear chessboard of the 1990's, where submarines under the ice could launch missiles after reductions are made in land-based missile systems. For years the Finns have worried that the Norwegians and the Soviets might accidentally collide in the Barents Sea and catch Finland in between. President Kekkonen proposed a nuclear-free Arctic zone in the 1960's, but though the Canadians are also concerned, the Arctic has not been included in recent disarmament negotiations.

New Trade Dynamics

Now that Finland has attained a secure and stable place, the world is changing rapidly around it. Under the impact of *glasnost*, the new Soviet "openness" policy, West European countries and the U.S.S.R. are seeking greater contact and trade, which could lessen the Soviets' interest in their special trade relationship with Finland.

Europe is in a historic period in which every aspect of doing business is going to change. The twelve nations of the European Community (EC) are expecting to remove trade barriers separating them in late 1992. At that time the EC will become a single market of 320 million consumers living in Belgium, Britain, Denmark, France, Germany, Greece, Ireland, Italy, Luxembourg, Netherlands, Portugal, and Spain. Finland, Sweden, and other neutral countries are worried about how to maintain their neutrality while still trading with a unified European community, and about whether new barriers will exist for those outside the group.

Finland will have to maneuver with skill and ingenuity to fit into the world markets of the mid-1990's. As a small country, it cannot hope to compete with giant producers and instead has selected several areas in which to excel. Finland's largest independent firm, Nokia, for example, is the biggest personal computer and color television manufacturer in all of Scandinavia and is hoping for breakthroughs into wider markets. Such expansion for Finnish business is the newest challenge, but then Finns are used to challenges.

Third World Connections

In 1986–1987 the Finnish Ministry of Education announced a plan to establish a professorship in East Asian languages and cultures at the University of Helsinki, to be followed by a program leading to the teaching of thirty-five non-European languages by 1995. Many connect this trend with the critical need to develop more trade with the markets of Asia, Africa, the Middle East, and Latin America.

Politicians are rethinking Finland's relationships with the Third World. One day they debate the foreign aid budget and how many refugees they can incorporate into their "small, poor country," and the next day they realize they are no longer so poor.

Finnish Identity

As English becomes the language many Finns use in international markets, and as Finnish companies develop subsidiaries with non-Finnish employees, there is increasing concern that the "home" culture will disappear. As American fast-food chains and television series, along with European satellite broadcasts, internationalize Finnish "youth culture," and as Finland experiences its first generation of "juppies" (spelled with a *J* but meaning and sounding the same as yuppies), some pessimists argue that commercialism will erase what it is to be Finnish.

Lest the old work ethic and closeness to nature be forgotten, students from Helsinki spend time on farms each spring.   Hannu Vanhanen

People fear that consumerism is eroding the old values of simple dignity and self-reliance. Meanwhile, students debate why Finnish pedestrians stop at red lights when there are no cars and it is –20° F. (–30° C.), and why Finns have trouble drinking in moderation.

As Finns increase their travel and business ties with Western Europe, they have begun to see themselves as more a part of Europe than as an isolated periphery. Physical anthropologists have begun to stress the Finn's Nordic heritage, and linguists are in doubt about what conclusions can really be drawn from the similarity between Finnish and the Siberian languages.

While Finland expands its ties abroad, it is also turning inward and reasserting its identity as a Nordic country. It continues to strengthen its links with the other member states of the Nordic Council. Finns look to their history of national struggle and seek to build a new strength as a neutral meeting ground contributing quietly to world stability.

Finns no longer stress *sisu*, the *Kalevala*, or Sibelius as much as in the past. The sauna is still exported, even to Lebanon with the Finnish U.N. troops, and Finnish national independence and individual stubbornness are still celebrated. In spite of all the technological advances, an Arctic freeze can still slow the country down; in spite of all the political trends toward consensus, a strike can still stop communications; in spite of all the changes since it declared its independence in 1917, Finland can be described as a spunky little nation that still has wilderness, courage, and dreams.

Bibliography

A. General

Facts About Finland. Helsinki: Otava Publishing Company, 1987. A basic handbook introduction to Finnish geography, history, government, economy, and culture, including "Who's Who in Finland" with 70 entries.

Mead, W. F. *Finland.* Nations of the Modern World Series. New York: Praeger Publishers, Inc., 1968. A general book by a British social geographer with much experience in Finland. For the advanced student.

Nickels, Sylvie, ed. *Finland: An Introduction.* New York: Praeger Publishers, Inc., 1973. A series of brief essays by Finns and Britons on history, politics, farming, the church, architecture, design, etc. Extensive bibliography.

Rajanen, Aini. *Of Finnish Ways.* Minneapolis: Dillon Press, Inc., 1981. A conversational-style description of Finnish history and culture through the eyes of a Finnish American. Recipes; selected bibliography.

Screen, J. E. P. *Finland.* World Bibliographical Series. Santa Barbara, CA: Clio Press, 1981. An excellent annotated bibliography of books in English on Finland.

Stoddard, Theodore Lothrop. *Area Handbook for Finland.* Washington, D.C.: American University Press, 1974. An overview of Finnish language, history, politics, literature, etc. For the advanced student.

B. The Northern Setting (Chapter 2)

Hautala, Hannu. *A Year in Kuusamo: Diary of a Finnish Bird Photographer.* Espoo: Weilin ja Göös, 1985. Chosen the Nature Book of the Year in 1984 by the World Wildlife Fund of Finland; dramatically illustrates how birds adapt to the different seasons in a municipality in the northeast.

C. The People (Chapter 3)

Flint, Aili. *Say It in Finnish.* New York: Dover Publications, Inc., 1983. A useful phrase book with a brief introduction to the language.

Karlsson, Fred. *Finnish Grammar*, translated by Andrew Chesterman. Helsinki: Werner Söderström Osakeyhtiö, 1983. For foreigners wanting to learn the basics of grammar or linguistics students interested in the structure of Finnish. The author is professor of general linguistics at the University of Helsinki.

Manker, Ernst. *People of Eight Seasons.* New York: Crescent Books, a division of Crown Publishers, Inc., 1963. A discussion of Sami prehistory and history by a senior curator at the Nordic Museum in Stockholm, followed by an account of the annual cycle in eight seasons: early spring, spring, early summer, summer, late summer, autumn, late autumn, winter. Dramatic black-and-white sketches and diagrams; a few colored photos; select bibliography.

Pitkanen, Matti A. and Ilkka. *Poromiehet: The Lapps and Their Reindeer.* Espoo: Weilin ja Göös, 1984. Stunning photographs and vivid account of the life of reindeer herders, based on interviews mostly in Finland from 1978 to 1983.

Vuorela, Toivo. *The Finno-Ugric Peoples.* Uralic and Altaic Series, Vol. 39. Blooming-ton, IN: Indiana University Press, 1964. Cultural history of the Finns, the Lapps, the Karelians, and ten other Finno-Ugric peoples, including the Estonians and Hungarians. Somewhat difficult, but interesting photos and sketches of "material culture": hats, plows, etc.

D. Geographical Regions (Chapters 4–7)
General

Havas, Paavo. *Land of Light: Northern Pictures.* Helsinki: Kirjayhtymä Oy, 1983. A description of the flora and fauna, with a discussion of adaptation from the rocky archipelago to the rockfaces of Lapland. Stunning color photos.

John, Brian Stephen. *Scandinavia: A New Geography.* New York: Longman, Green & Co., Inc., 1981; London: Longman Group Ltd., 1984. A solid general social geogra-phy text on all the Scandinavian countries: Iceland, Denmark, Norway, Sweden, and Finland.

North

See Hautala (B. Chapter 2) and Manker (C. Chapter 3).

Lakes

Lander, Patricia Slade. *In the Shadow of the Factory: Social Change in a Finnish Community.* New York: A Halsted Press Book, John Wiley & Sons/Schenkman Publication, 1976. A community study stressing social and political organization of a small factory town surrounded by farms in the north Savo area of the Lake District.

Coast See Mead (A. General).

Archipelago

Dreijer, Matts. *The History of the Åland People*, Vol. 1: "From the Stone Age to Gustavus Vasa," translated from the Swedish by Jocelyn Palmer. Stockholm: The Cultural Foundation of Åland (distributed by Almqvist & Wiksell International), 1986. A very detailed history by the former official archaeologist of Åland, sponsored by the Cultural Foundation of Åland. First of several planned volumes.

E. History (Chapters 8–12)

Engle, Eloise, and Lauri Paananen. *The Winter War: The Russo-Finnish Conflict, 1939–1940.* New York: Charles Scribner's Sons, 1973. A very readable account of the day-to-day events on the front lines. Paananen served in the Home Guard in Tampere during the Winter War at the age of 15, surviving at least a dozen bombings of the city.

Hoglund, A. William. *Finnish Immigrants in America, 1880–1920.* Madison, WI: University of Wisconsin Press, 1960. The standard history of those who left for "the other side" during times of poverty and oppression.

Jacobson, Max. *Finland Survived: An Account of the Finnish-Soviet Winter War, 1939–1940*, 2nd ed. Helsinki: Otava Publishing Company, 1984. An important study by one of Finland's leading experts on international affairs, nominated by the Scandinavian governments to the post of Secretary-General of the U.N. and now head of the Council of Economic Organizations in Finland. For the advanced student.

Kirby, D. J. *Finland in the Twentieth Century.* Minneapolis: University of Minnesota Press, 1979. A historical account of Finland's economic and political development from 1900 to 1975 by British historian. For the advanced student.

Kivikoski, E. *Finland: Ancient People and Places.* New York: Praeger Publishers, Inc., 1967. The basic archaeological reference book in English; in need of some updating but still a good introduction.

Klinge, Matti. *A Brief History of Finland.* Helsinki: Otava Publishing Company, 1987. From the Ice Age to the 1980's: a good starting point.

Mannerheim, C. G. E. *The Memoirs of Marshal Mannerheim.* New York: E. P. Dutton, 1954. One of the most important figures in Finnish history from the Civil War through his brief presidency, 1944–1946.

Paasilinna, Arto. *Illustrated Episodes in a 10,000 Year Odyssey: A Businessman's Guide to Finnish History*, illustrated by Hannu Lukkarinen, translated by Gregory Coogan. Helsinki: Business Books/Uusi Suomi Oy, 1986. An excellent and interesting book, which gives an account of Finnish history through the eyes of fictional characters, stressing the struggle and violence. May be difficult to find in the United States— ask your library to order it from the Academic Bookstore, Keskuskatu 1, SF-00100 Helsinki 10, Finland, the largest bookstore in Finland.

Wuorinen, John H. *A History of Finland.* New York: Published for the American-Scandinavian Foundation by Columbia University Press, 1965. A detailed history through 1962 by a Finnish-American historian.

F. Democratic Traditions (Chapter 13)

Arter, David. *Politics and Policy-Making in Finland.* New York: St. Martin's Press, 1987. A complex political-science treatise with very good recent data for the advanced student.

Gripenberg, Alexandra. *A Half Year in the New World: Miscellaneous Sketches of Travel in the United States (1888)*, translated and edited by Ernest J. Moyne. Newark, DE: University of Delaware Press, 1954. The account of one of Europe's leading feminists, who attended the first International Council of Women in 1888 in Washington, D.C., and then traveled from coast to coast observing American life before returning to Finland to become the President of the Finnish Women's Association from 1889 to 1903.

Haavio-Mannila, Elina, et al., eds. *Unfinished Democracy: Women in Nordic Politics.* Elmsford, NY: Pergamon Press, Inc., 1985. Detailed analysis of women's organizations, and of participation in elections, in Parliament, in local politics, and in the corporate system, coming to the conclusion that "politics is still a man's world, although not nearly as exclusively as it was a century ago." For the advanced student. Excellent bibliography.

Rintala, Marvin. *Four Finns: Political Profiles.* Berkeley, CA: University of California Press, 1969. Interesting account of "four men among many": "The Aristocrat in Politics"—Gustaf Mannerheim; "The Bureaucrat in Politics"—Väinö Tanner; "The Scholar in Politics"—K. J. Ståhlberg; "The Politician in Politics"—J. K. Paasikivi.

G. Literature (Chapter 14)

Laitinen, Kai. *Literature of Finland: An Outline.* Helsinki: Otava Publishing Company,

1985. A short but thorough survey of Finnish literature from the Middle Ages to the present.

Selected Literature in Translation

Dauenhauer, Richard, and Philip Binham. *Snow in May: An Anthology of Finnish Writing, 1945–1972*. Rutherford, NJ: Fairleigh Dickinson University Press, 1978. The first major anthology of Finnish literature (from Finnish- and Swedish-language authors) in translation: poems, short stories, and Eeva-Liisa Manner's play *Snow in May*. Nine brief essays on Finnish literature. Selected bibliography of translated works.

Heikkila, Ritva, ed. *Minna Canth—Pioneer Reformer. Minna Canth's Works and Letters (Sanoi Minna Canth. Otteita Minna Canthin teoksista ja kirjeista)*. Helsinki: Werner Söderström Osakeyhtiö, 1987. A selection of extracts from the writings of Finland's champion of social reforms; in Finnish and in English translation.

Jansson, Tove. *Moomintroll books* (a series of seven). New York: Avon Books, 1971.

Kivi, Aleksis. *Seven Brothers*. New York: The American-Scandinavian Foundation, 1962.

Linna, Väinö. *The Unknown Soldier*. New York: G. P. Putnam's Sons, 1957; Helsinki: Werner Söderström Osakeyhtiö, 1970.

Lönnrot, Elias. *The Kalevala*, translated by Francis P. Magoun, Jr. Cambridge, Mass.: Harvard University Press, 1963. Considered by many the best English translation.

Meri, Veijo. *The Manila Rope*. New York: Alfred A. Knopf, Inc., 1967.

Pekkanen, Toivo. *My Childhood*. Madison, WI: University of Wisconsin Press, 1966.

Saarikoski, Pentti. *Helsinki: Selected Poems of Pentti Saarikoski*. Chicago: Swall Press, 1967.

Sillanpää, Frans Eemil. *People in the Summer Night*. Madison, WI: University of Wisconsin Press, 1966.

———. *Meek Heritage*. Helsinki: Otava Publishing Company, 1971.

Waltari, Mika. Over a dozen novels have been translated into English. The first was *The Adventurer*. New York: G. P. Putnam's Sons, 1950.

English Novels with a Finnish Background

Gavin, Catherine. *The Fortress*. London: Hodder & Stoughton, Ltd., 1964. A historical novel of Suomenlinna during the Crimean War.

Kurten, Bjørn. *The Dance of the Tiger*. New York: Pantheon Books, 1980. The novel by the Finland-Swedish paleontologist describes the conflict between the Neanderthal and Cro-Magnon populations along the coastal area of Finland and Sweden during one of the milder periods of the last Ice Age.

———. *Singletusk—An Ice Age Novel.* New York: Pantheon Books, 1984.

Lyall, Gavine. *The Most Dangerous Game.* London: Hodder & Stoughton, Ltd.; New York: Macfadden-Bartell Corp., 1964. A mystery set in Finnish Lapland.

H. Music, Architecture, and Design (Chapter 15)

Music

Layton, Robert. *Sibelius and His World.* New York: A Studio Book/Viking Press, 1970. An interesting biography with attention to Sibelius' social surroundings. Many photos; chronology.

Richards, Denby. *The Music of Finland.* London: Hugh Evelyn, 1968. A stress on music after Sibelius.

Architecture and Design

Gaynor, Elizabeth. *Finland: Living Design.* 480 photographs by Kari Haavisto. New York: Rizzoli, 1984. An important book for understanding Finnish architecture and design in its historical and ecological context. Includes Karelian and Lapp homes and clothes. Strikingly beautiful color photographs.

Helander, Vilhelm, and Simo Rista. *Modern Architecture in Finland/Suomalainen Rakennustaide.* Helsinki: Kirjayhtymä Oy, 1987. A richly illustrated book that presents the classical works by Alvar Aalto but also the less-well-known work of Reima Pietilä and others.

Richards, J. M. *Eight Hundred Years of Finnish Architecture.* London: David & Charles, 1978. Describes the development of Finnish architecture from the ancient castles and medieval village churches to the work of Alvar Aalto. Photographs.

Schildt, Gøran. *Alvar Aalto, The Early Years.* New York: Rizzoli, 1984.

———. *Alvar Aalto, The Decisive Years.* New York: Rizzoli, 1986. First two of three volumes; fascinating accounts of the life of Aalto by the leading authority on Aalto and an acquaintance of thirty years.

I. Holidays (Chapter 16)

Lipsanen, Anneke. *The Finnish Folk Year: A Perpetual Diary and Book of Days, Ways, and Customs.* Helsinki: Otava Publishing Company, 1987. An interesting month-by-month account of old and new customs and artifacts.

Ojakangas, Beatrice A. *The Finnish Cookbook.* International Cookbook Series. New York: Crown Publishers, Inc., 1964. A Finnish-American went to Finland in 1960–1961 and recorded 400 recipes from all regions and adapted them to American measurements.

Viherjuuri, H. J. *Sauna, the Finnish Bath.* Helsinki: Otava Publishing Company, 1967. History and techniques of sauna bathing.

Magazines and Pamphlets

A special issue of *Scandinavian Review* (Vol. 75, No. 4: December 1987), in honor of the 70th anniversary of Finnish independence; has articles from politics to art.

Books from Finland. A magazine in English published by Helsinki University Library four times a year. Includes articles, short book reviews, and translations of current Finnish writers. Available from P.O. Box 312, SF-00171 Helsinki, Finland.

Fennia. Journal of the Finnish Geographical Society. A wide range of articles on climate, rocks, settlement patterns, etc. In major libraries.

Finland in Figures. Annual. Available from Central Statistical Office of Finland, P.O. Box 504, SF-00101 Helsinki, Finland.

Finnish Features. A set of short pamphlets or "fact sheets" on a wide range of topics from history to sports, published by the Ministry for Foreign Affairs. Two included in the set are "The Roots of the Finnish Language" and "Swedish Finland." Available from the Finnish Embassy, Washington, D.C., or the Ministry for Foreign Affairs, Lönnrotinkatu 4-B, SF-00120 Helsinki, Finland.

Filmography

A number of 16mm. films and VHS video cassettes are available from the Consulate General of Finland (540 Madison Avenue, New York, N.Y. 10022; phone 212 832–6550) on a free-loan basis. Reservations should be made at least two weeks in advance. This is a partial list:

A Lakeside Road in Finland. 16mm. 34 minutes. On the evolution of an artists' colony when Finland was struggling for national independence.

Åland. VHS. 22 minutes. Life in the Åland Islands: the archipelago, nature, seafaring, fishing, history, and tourism.

A Sparrow on Christmas Morning. VHS. 37 minutes. The Finnish Brass Band and soprano Karita Mattila perform Finnish Christmas songs in the old stone church of Porvoo.

Finnovations. VHS. 15 minutes. Narrated by David Frost. On Finnish technology and industry today and Finns as solution finders.

Roots of a Republic. 16mm or VHS. 30 minutes. On Finnish political history. Winner of the State Film Award, 1985.

The Finnish Solution. VHS. Examines Finnish political history. Produced by the University of North Carolina Center for Public Television, 1987.

Other Films

Finland's countryside has been the backdrop for some foreign films, e.g., *Dr. Zhivago*, and for Finland's own film industry.

The classic war novel by Väinö Linna, *Tuntematon sotilas* (*The Unknown Soldier*), was made into a film by Edvin Laine in the 1950's and remade by Rauni Mollberg in 1985 in Finland.

Discography

Jazz

Recently a dozen or more records of Finnish jazz have been recorded. A new group, The Jari Perkkiomäki Quartet, recorded its own compositions ("Cartolina," "Ballad," "Opus 113," "Flyer with the Roof Slightly Higher," "Mr. CC," "Hymn") in February 1985 as *Acoustic Jazz*. Kompass Records KOLP 64.

Jean Sibelius

Finlandia, op. 26 (orchestra). Finlandia Records FACD 002, 005.

Two never-before-recorded string quartets: *String Quartets in A minor (1889)* and *B Flat Major (1890)*. The Sibelius Academy Quartet. Finlandia Records FAD 345 (1985).

Works for Piano, Vols. 1 and 2. Cyril Szalkiewicz, piano. Finlandia Records FA 802 and 804.

Opera

Kokkonen, Joonas. *Viimeiset Kiusaukset* (*The Last Temptations*). Opera in two acts. Savonlinna Opera Festival Chorus and Orchestra, Ulf Söderblom, conductor. Finlandia Records FA 104 LP3.

Sallinen, Aulis. *Ratsumies* (*The Horseman*). Opera in three acts. Savonlinna Opera Festival Chorus and Orchestra, Ulf Söderblom, conductor. Finlandia Records FA 101 LP3.

―――. *Punainen viiva* (*The Red Line*). Opera in two acts. Finnish National Opera Chorus and Orchestra, Okko Kamu, conductor. Finlandia Records FA 102 LP3.

The young Finnish conductor Esa-Pekka Salonen has recently received international renown. He has been the principal conductor of the Swedish Radio Orchestra and principal guest conductor of the London Philharmonia and Oslo Philharmonic. He has recorded almost a dozen albums for CBS Records, including music of Sibelius, Nielsen, Messiaen, and Lutoslawski.

Folk Music

Finnish Folk Dances. A collection of 17 Finnish folk dances, including several quadrilles, waltzes, and polkas, and a polska. Finnlevy (contact World Tone Music, 230 7th Avenue, NYC 10011).

Finnish Folk Songs. Martti Talvela, Bass. Finlandia Records, FAD 917.

Index

Numbers in *italics* refer to illustrations.